BOWLING

Steps to Success

Robert H. Strickland, MS
Dallas, Texas

Leisure Press
Champaign, Illinois

Library of Congress Cataloging-in-Publication Data

Strickland, Robert.
   Bowling : steps to success.

   (Steps to success activity series)
   Bibliography: p.
   1. Bowling. I. Title. II. Series.
GV903.S76 1989   794.6   88-37740
ISBN 0-88011-355-3

ISBN: 0-88011-355-3

Developmental Editor: Judy Patterson Wright, PhD
Production Director: Ernie Noa
Copy Editor: Peter Nelson
Assistant Editors: Holly Gilly and Robert King
Proofreader: Laurie McGee
Typesetter: Yvonne Winsor
Text Design: Keith Blomberg
Text Layout: Jayne Clampitt
Cover Design: Jack Davis
Cover Photo: Bill Morrow
Illustrations By: Raneé Rogers and Gretchen Walters
Printed By: United Graphics, Inc.

Printed in the United States of America

10 9 8 7 6 5 4 3 2 1

Leisure Press
A Division of Human Kinetics Publishers, Inc.
Box 5076, Champaign, IL 61825-5076
1-800-747-4457

10 9 8 7 6 5 4 3 2

Contents

Series Preface

The Steps to Success Activity Series is a breakthrough in skill instruction through the development of complete learning progressions—the *steps to success*. These *steps* help students quickly perform basic skills successfully and prepare them to acquire advanced skills readily. At each step, students are encouraged to learn at their own pace and to integrate their new skills into the total action of the activity, which motivates them to achieve.

The unique features of the Steps to Success Activity Series are the result of comprehensive development—through analyzing existing activity books, incorporating the latest research from the sport sciences, and consulting with students, instructors, teacher educators, and administrators. This groundwork pointed up the need for three different types of books—for participants, instructors, and teacher educators—which we have created and together comprise the Steps to Success Activity Series.

The *participant's book* for each activity is a self-paced, step-by-step guide; learners can use it as a primary resource for a beginning activity class or as a self-instructional guide. The unique features of each *step* in the participant's book include

- sequential illustrations that clearly show proper technique for all basic skills,
- helpful suggestions for detecting and correcting errors,
- excellent drill progressions with accompanying *Success Goals* for measuring performance, and
- a complete checklist for each basic skill for a trained observer to rate the learner's technique.

A comprehensive *instructor's guide* accompanies the participant's book for each activity, emphasizing how to individualize instruction. Each *step* of the instructor's guide promotes successful teaching and learning with

- teaching cues (*Keys to Success*) that emphasize fluidity, rhythm, and wholeness,
- criterion-referenced rating charts for evaluating a participant's initial skill level,
- suggestions for observing and correcting typical errors,
- tips for group management and safety,
- ideas for adapting every drill to increase or decrease the difficulty level,
- quantitative evaluations for all drills (*Success Goals*), and
- a complete test bank of written questions.

The series textbook, *Instructional Design for Teaching Physical Activities*, explains the *steps to success* model, which is the basis for the Steps to Success Activity Series. Teacher educators can use this text in their professional preparation classes to help future teachers and coaches learn how to design effective physical activity programs in school, recreation, or community teaching and coaching settings.

After identifying the need for participant, instructor, and teacher educator texts, we refined the *steps to success* instructional design model and developed prototypes for the participant's book and the instructor's guide. Once these prototypes were fine-tuned, we carefully selected authors for the activities who were not only thoroughly familiar with their sports but also had years of experience in teaching them. Each author had to be known as a gifted instructor who understands the teaching of sport so thoroughly that he or she could readily apply the *steps to success* model.

Next, all of the participant's and instructor's manuscripts were carefully developed to meet the guidelines of the *steps to success* model. Then our production team, along with outstanding artists, created a highly visual, user-friendly series of books.

The result: The Steps to Success Activity Series is the premier sports instructional series available today. The participant's books are the best available for helping you to become a master player, the instructor's guides will help you to become a master teacher, and the teacher educator's text prepares you to design your own programs.

This series would not have been possible without the contributions of the following:

- Dr. Joan Vickers, instructional design expert,
- Dr. Rainer Martens, Publisher,
- the staff of Human Kinetics Publishers, and
- the *many* students, teachers, coaches, consultants, teacher educators, specialists, and administrators who shared their ideas—and dreams.

Judy Patterson Wright
Series Editor

From the developmental and competitive phases of my own bowling career I can recall many times when I needed to know certain facts and techniques: how to execute a movement, how to practice more productively, how to organize my thoughts and actions for success during competition. Because standard texts provided few answers, my needs were unfulfilled until I got a tip from an experienced bowler or stumbled onto a successful technique after hours, days, weeks, or even months of frustrating trial and error.

Bowling: Steps to Success is a collection of facts, tips, and techniques arranged in a sequence to enable you to apply bowling skills effectively when you need them during practice. Goal-oriented drills help you quickly ingrain the feel of efficient movements into your muscles. You will learn to troubleshoot your own performance through comparing your movements to how the correct ones feel. You will become skilled at executing a free-pendulum swing and the four-step delivery. You will learn effective strike and spare targeting as well as mental practice skills. Many of the drills utilize a buddy system so you and your lanemates can help each other learn quickly.

Bowling: Steps to Successs should be your constant companion during practice. If you are a beginner, you should use it to learn correct form and techniques from the start. If you are already a skilled bowler, you should use it to systematically break out of slumps and eliminate bad habits while filling the holes in your knowledge and simplifying your bowling form.

Thanks to Wilson G. ''Bill'' Taylor for many of the techniques included in this book. Our many discussions and workouts helped me understand and feel elements of bowling form more deeply. His teaching strategies utilizing the extension setup, the assisted balance arm, the finish, and the footwork drill are major contributions to this book and to students of bowling. Without his assistance, I could not have written *Bowling: Steps to Success*.

Thanks to my wife, Sue, for her loving support, for posing for many of the photographs for the illustrator to work from, and for critically evaluating the manuscript. Thanks to Pete Moore, member of the Dallas Bowling Association Hall of Fame, for the loan of special camera equipment, for his always-helpful suggestions, and for proofreading the galleys. Thanks to David Brewster, Myra Lachausse, and Manuel San Miguel for posing for photographs for the illustrator to work from, and for their helpful suggestions on how to improve them. Lastly, thanks to Glenn Scifres for suggesting the term ''low maintenance game.''

Robert H. Strickland

The Steps to Success Staircase

Get ready to climb a staircase—one that will lead you to become an accomplished bowler. You cannot leap to the top; you get there by climbing one step at a time.

Each of the 16 steps you will take is an easy transition from the one before. The first few steps of the staircase provide a solid foundation of basic skills and concepts. As you progress further, you will learn how to connect groups of those seemingly isolated skills. You will learn how to consistently make strikes, convert spares, mentally prepare, and adapt to various game situations. As you near the top of the staircase, you will become more confident in your ability to be successful in many different contexts—practice, league, and tournament play.

Familiarize yourself with this section as well as the ''The Sport of Bowling,'' ''Selecting Your Equipment,'' and ''Preparing Your Body for Success,'' sections for an orientation and in order to understand how to set up your practice sessions around the steps.

Follow the same sequence each step (chapter) of the way:

1. Read the explanations of what is covered in the step, why the step is important, and how to execute or perform the step's focus, which may be on basic skills, concepts, tactics or a combination of the three.

2. Follow the numbered illustrations showing exactly how to position your body to execute each basic skill successfully. There are three general parts to each skill: preparation (getting into a starting position), execution (performing the skill that is the focus of the step), and recovery (reaching a finish position or following through to starting position).

3. Look over the common errors that may occur and the recommendations for how to correct them.

4. The drills help you improve your skills through repetition and purposeful practice. Read the directions and the Success Goal for each drill. Practice accordingly and record your scores. Compare your score with the Success Goal for the drill. You need to meet the Success Goal of each drill before moving on to practice the next one because the drills are arranged in an easy-to-difficult progression. This sequence is designed specifically to help you achieve continual success.

5. As soon as you can reach all the Success Goals for one step, you are ready for a qualified observer—such as your teacher, coach, or trained partner—to evaluate your basic skill technique against the Keys to Success Checklist. This is a qualitative or subjective evaluation of your basic technique or form, because using correct form can enhance your performance. Your evaluator can tailor specific goals for you, if they are needed, by using the Individual Program form (see Appendix A). There is also a blank scoresheet for recording practice games in Appendix B.

6. Repeat these procedures for each of the 16 Steps to Success. Then rate yourself according to the directions in the ''Rating Your Total Progress'' section.

Good luck on your step-by-step journey to developing your bowling skills, building confidence, experiencing success, and having fun!

The Sport of Bowling

Bowling can be traced back at least 7,000 years to Egypt, where archeologists unearthed stone balls and nine pins from a child's gravesite. Bowling's history for the next 5,000 years is largely unknown.

In third-century Germany, bowling was a religious rite. At that time, Germans carried clubs called *kegels* for protection. At one end of the church cloister they would stand up a kegel to symbolize a heathen and roll a ball at it from the other end. If a bowler (*kegler*) knocked over the kegel, he was said to have killed the heathen and was honored at a post-session banquet. Any bowler failing to knock over the kegel was encouraged to seek spiritual fortification in church.

For the next thousand years, Germans bowled at clusters of 3 to 17 pins; 9 emerged as the most popular number. Play was commonly conducted on such diverse surfaces as clay, slate, and cinders, with the wooden surface first appearing in Holland and Switzerland. The bowling playing surface of this time was approximately 1 foot wide.

Ninepin bowling was simultaneously spreading to France, England, and Spain, but with varied pin arrangements and widely diverse pin dimensions. The French had *quilles*, and the English had skittles and long-bowling, the forerunner of the modern game of bowling.

In England, bowling assumed the character of a commoners' sport, the first public establishment being opened in London in the fifteenth century. The word *alley* became associated with pin bowling establishments, and bowling became more closely identified with tavern life. It was with this image that bowling came to America with the Dutch colonists.

Allen (1986) divides the evolution of bowling in America into four general time periods based upon the organization of participation, the establishment of standards for play, and on the localization of control into various guiding bodies. The *developmental era* (1837-1875) featured bowling's growth as a regular outdoor family activity for German immigrant social groups. Eventually participation moved indoors to ethnic cultural centers in which persons of similar background could enjoy food, drink, and recreational activities together. In 1840 America's first commercial indoor establishment, the Knickerbocker Alleys, opened in Manhattan, featuring ninepin bowling. This venture enjoyed continued success primarily because it served the desires of New York's large German population. Soon the outward enthusiasm of these people for bowling attracted other Americans to the sport.

Bowling continued to draw gamblers and hustlers, and genuine bowling enthusiasts waged continuous battles against local authorities who tried to ban bowling activity as a way to eliminate gambling, the idle use of time, and drinking. It is believed that the addition of a 10th pin to the pin arrangement was a tactic to circumvent an 1837 ban of public ninepin bowling by the government of Connecticut.

As public bans on leisure activities became more frequent, bowling groups answered the challenge by forming clubs. Such clubs were legally protected as long as they were appropriately licensed and originated for the common good of the members. During the *club era* (1875-1895), the exclusive but permissive club environment provided a way for serious enthusiasts to shape the development of bowling in America. Bowling's continued existence was assured within the confines of the club, but the chaotic state of playing rules and standards left the future of large-scale competitive bowling uncertain. Bowling took many forms: Bowlers of the East played by different rules than did bowlers of the West; some bowled ninepins, whereas others bowled tenpins.

During these years, a maximum score was usually 200, with three balls allowed per *frame* (each attempt to knock down a full setup of pins) and 10 frames making up one game. In some areas, a bowler started with 200 points, and points were deducted with each roll of the ball, the objective being to be the first to reach zero. Fallen pins were sometimes left on the lane, sometimes swept off before the next ball was rolled. Further, the size and weight of balls and pins varied greatly, and there were no standards concerning lane specifications.

Uniform rules and standards were absolutely vital for bowling to grow and for the beginning of nationwide competition. In an effort to foster competitive bowling, bowling clubs formed umbrella organizations for the purpose of imposing rules and standards to which all participants could adhere. These governing bodies were not cohesive enough to survive, but each made some contribution to the overall goal of standardization. The first such group, made up of members of several clubs, appeared in 1875; it was called the National Bowling Association (NBA). The NBA formulated rules with respect to ball size, playing procedures, and lane dimensions. In 1890 the American Bowling League (ABL), successor to the NBA, standardized pin size and eliminated the third ball from the frame, but left the maximum possible score at 200.

The *competitive era* (1895-1961) featured the most remarkable growth of competitive bowling. It began with the formation of the American Bowling Congress (ABC), with which most league bowlers are familiar today. In 1895 this body agreed upon the present method of scoring with 300 as a maximum score, which gave the bowler more room for improvement. It also agreed upon the current 12-inch center-to-center spacing of pins and initiated a program of lane inspection to ensure consistency with adopted specifications.

The ABC also started a yearly tournament to promote the sport and allow persons from all parts of the nation to compete with each other under standardized conditions. Two such tournaments exist today: the ABC Tournament for men and the WIBC (Women's International Bowling Congress) Tournament for women. Each features scratch competition in singles, doubles, and five-member team events.

As bowling began to provide great fame and monetary reward, skilled bowlers were often featured in match game competition. They would barnstorm through the country with their financial backers, often taking on all challengers in their own (*home*) establishments—

which were often filled to capacity. Because these matches involved wagering, the bigger the crowd, the more intense the betting action. A big draw was advantageous to the proprietor, who sold more food and drink; to the traveling star and his group, who were paid for the appearance; and to all gamblers, who stood better chances in a larger crowd to diversify bets.

Naturally there was a tremendous commercial advantage in being designated "the best." Many claimed to be the "best bowler in America" or "the best bowler in the world." Such claims became so careless and widespread that the *challenge match system* became a way to determine who really was the best. Challenge matches followed most of the several large tournaments that were held around the country, but there were no formal schedules like we see in professional bowling today. Skilled bowlers simply participated in as many of these tournaments as they could. The person with the best winning record had the right to claim the national match game championship or to challenge the current champion to a series of match games, during which the title could change hands. The winner of the challenge match was then obliged to defend his title against other worthy opponents.

The challenge method was discarded in favor of the All-Star tournament, for which participants had to qualify through a system of local and state competition. The All-Star was later joined by a similar tournament, the World's Invitational, to which bowlers were invited. Women's divisions were added later. These tournaments served nicely to determine the best in the *field* (total group of participants) by running them through the difficult paces of a 100-game format!

Because of extensive television exposure in the late 1950s and early 1960s, bowling experienced a sharp rise in popularity with people of all ages. This bowling boom accounted for the appearance of many large bowling centers around the country, wherein bowling was given its finishing touches as a full-blown family recreation. The Professional Bowlers Association (PBA) was founded in 1958, emphasizing scratch singles competition for skilled bowlers. Its continuing television coverage and that of the Ladies' Professional Bowlers Tour (LPBT) keep bowling in the public eye.

The *commercial era* (1961 to the present) is characterized by the deemphasis of the sport image of bowling in favor of a recreational image. The bowling industry feels that its interests are best served by promoting bowling as an easily learned recreational activity. This attitude is reflected in the active marketing of high-velocity pins, the increased elasticity of bowling balls, and conditioning lane surfaces to promote high scoring. The game of the present era, although less demanding in accuracy than the game of the 1940s and 1950s, is still America's most popular communal sport.

CONDUCT

Courtesy and *sportsmanship* are inseparable concepts that are absolutely essential in the bowling environment. Courtesy and sportsmanship must both exist for all competitors to enjoy peak performance! All bowlers must work together to ensure the right of each and every participant to be as good as his or her ability will allow.

Here are some ways in which you can help yourself and others:

1. *Respect the equipment.* Do not *loft* the ball, tossing it far out onto the lane surface; it will make a pock mark in the lane. Do not kick the ball return. Do not roll a second ball until your first one has returned; you may find yourself liable for any damages that occur to expensive equipment. Also, do not use another person's ball without permission. Keep all personal items, especially bowling balls and bags, off the seats and out of any traffic area.

2. *Respect the valuable time of your teammates and the proprietor* by being ready when it is your turn to bowl. Remain in and around the *settee* area until it is your turn to bowl; meet the person who bowls before you as he or she is stepping off the approach. During practice, take only one practice ball—not a whole frame—at a time. Then step aside, allowing the next person his or her practice ball. If you wait to roll a second ball, you deprive the bowlers

on your pair of lanes of approximately one third of their total practice time.

3. *Always allow the bowlers around you every chance to concentrate* on each shot. Yield to the bowler on your immediate left or right if he or she is ready to bowl. Do not distract anyone in the setup. Be quiet in and around your settee area. Avoid standing on the approach next to any bowler (an exception is made for anyone working out with an instructor or a partner in a class setting). Control your emotions by confining your movements to your approach, making no animated gestures when returning from the foul line and making no sudden noises at any time.

4. *Create a positive atmosphere.* Avoid wasting time on the approach, making excuses for poor bowling, bragging about your achievements, laughing at or berating others, needling any opponent, or using loud or vulgar language. Avoid saying anything negative or anxiety-causing to anyone—especially when he or she is returning from making a bad shot. Give no advice to anyone unless he or she has asked for advice.

GENERAL SAFETY TIPS

The bowling environment presents several possible dangers to the untrained bowler. Falling down is a hazard that can be minimized by making sure that there are no foreign substances on your shoes or on the approach. Follow these guidelines:

- Never apply powder or ashes to help you slide.
- Always keep food and drinks out of the bowling area.
- Never step beyond the foul line; you might track lane dressing back onto the approach.
- Never bowl in street shoes.
- Always check the bottoms of your shoes before bowling if you have walked out of the settee area for any reason.

Another potential danger is being hit with, or hitting someone else with, a bowling ball. Get in the habit of taking these precautions:

- Always look around you to see whether anyone is taking practice swings.

- Be careful with your own practice swings; always know how much room you have for making your movements. A good idea is to take practice swings or slides only on the approach and in the direction of the pins.
- Pick up your ball only on the sides, with both hands, and only after it has come to a stop on the ball return. You can avoid mashing your fingers if you look down at your ball as you pick it up with both hands (see Figures I.1a and b).

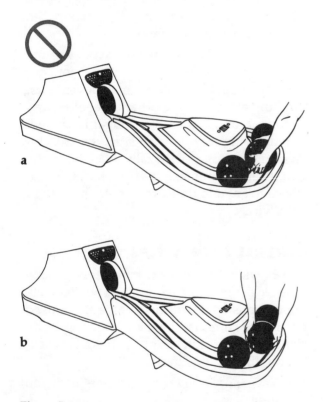

Figure I.1 Picking up a bowling ball: (a) improper technique risks smashed fingers; (b) proper technique ensures safety.

Finally, two very important warnings are as follows:

- Never—under any circumstance—trigger the pinsetting machine to operate if someone is working on it.
- Never—under any circumstance—roll a ball toward the pins if someone is working on the pinsetter or if the pins are not fully exposed and ready for the ball to be rolled.

HOW A GAME IS PLAYED

Tenpin bowling is a game played by *delivering* (rolling) a ball 27 inches in circumference (about 8-1/2 inches diameter) down an *alley*, or *lane*, 42 inches (39 boards) wide. The ball rolls 60 feet toward a *rack* (formation) of 10 pins. The pins, each 15 inches high, are set in an equilateral triangular formation, the center of one pin 12 inches from the next (see Figure I.2a and b). The primary objective is to *strike*—to knock down all of the pins with one delivery of the ball. If a strike does not occur, the secondary objective is to *spare*—to knock down all of the pins left standing after the first delivery with a second delivery of the ball. A *cumulative score* is kept.

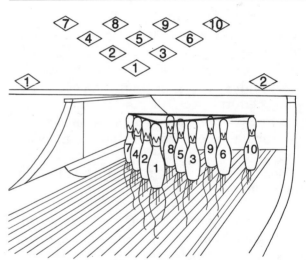

Figure I.2a A rack of tenpins.

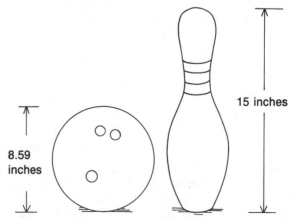

Figure I.2b Comparative dimensions of a bowling ball and a tenpin.

The bowler takes an *approach* within an area 15 feet by 42 inches also called the *approach*, or the *runway*. While delivering the ball, the bowler must not cross the *foul line*, the line that separates the approach from the lane proper. If the foul line is crossed, the delivery is declared illegal, and any pins knocked down count as zero. The bowler should also avoid rolling the ball into one of the 9-inch-wide *gutters*, or *channels*, on either side of the lane (see Figure I.3). Pins knocked down by a ball coming out of the channel do not count. See the current year's edition of the *American Bowling Congress Constitution, Specifications, Rules and Suggested League Rules Manual* for lane construction specifications.

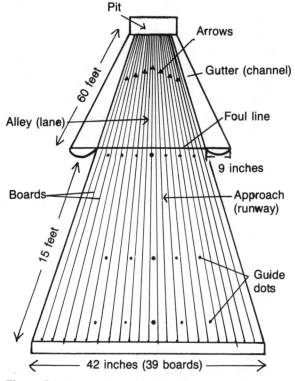

Figure I.3 Dimensions of a bowling lane and its approach.

TYPES OF GAME PLAY

There are several game contexts. The one in which beginners usually bowl is *open play*. This is self-paced, nonstructured bowling, not overseen or *sanctioned* by any organization. An example is someone dropping in to bowl a few games during the lunch hour. Open play may be recreational, which the bowler uses for relaxation, or serious practice, which features intense concentration on technique.

The opposite of open play is *competitive* bowling. It is divided into league and tournament competition, both of which are typically overseen by some governing organization, such as the ABC (men), the WIBC (women), or the Young American Bowling Alliance (YABA, for youngsters), to ensure compliance with rules and specifications. A competitive event may be exclusively limited to one sex; *mixed*, with both sexes in the same event; or one of various combinations of youngsters, adults, and senior citizens.

A league is a form of organized competition, with winners usually determined at the end of a 9-month bowling season. League play is most frequently conducted in the evening, and monetary prizes are awarded at the end of the league season. Recreational leagues feature small prizes; also, the great diversity of individual bowling skills often necessitates the addition of *handicap* (added pins) to scores. Serious competitive leagues feature larger prizes; there is less diversity of bowling skills, and competition is often conducted as *scratch* (without added handicap).

A tournament is similar to a league, with winners usually determined at the end of a single event. As in leagues, scores may be altered with handicap to encourage greater participation. There may be *medal* play, in which standings are decided by the score; *match* play, in which standings are decided by games or points won; or a combination of both, such as the point system used in PBA tournaments.

BASIC RULES AND SCORING

The following is a brief description of playing rules and scoring for the American game of tenpins. For a complete description of current tenpin bowling rules, regulations, and specifications, refer to the current year's edition of the *American Bowling Congress Constitution, Specifications, Rules and Suggested League Rules Manual*.

A game, or game score, of tenpin bowling consists of 10 *frames*. Each of the first 9 frames allows two deliveries; the 10th frame allows a third if the player makes a strike or a spare. A *legal delivery* is one in which the ball leaves the player's hand and touches the lane.

Legal pinfall may result from a legally delivered ball. Pins may be knocked down by the ball or by other pins rebounding from the *kickboards*, the side walls by the rack of pins; from the rear cushion behind the rack; or from the *sweep bar*, the horizontal bar that clears fallen pins off the *pin deck*, the part of the lane where the rack of pins is set (see Figure I.4). *Illegal pinfall* may also result from a legally delivered ball. Illegal pinfall does not count toward the score and may include pins knocked over by a ball that has left the lane before pin contact, pins knocked over by a ball rebounding from the rear cushion, or pins touched by a pinsetter before they fall. If a *foul* has been committed—some part of the bowler's body having touched the lane or any other portion of the bowling establishment past the foul line—any pinfall is illegal. Pins knocked down by a legal first ball in a frame and remaining on the playing surface are swept off so as not to interfere with a spare attempt at the standing pins.

A bowling score is *cumulative*, that is, pinfall from the current frame is added to that of the previous frames. The maximum score is 300, resulting from bonus pins being given for strikes and spares. (If scoring were simply additive, a maximum score for bowling would probably be between 100 and 240, depending upon whether 10 or 20 points were awarded for a strike and whether there were 10, 11, or 12 deliveries allowed.)

HOW TO KEEP SCORE

A *mark* refers to a strike (notated by an *X*) or a spare (a slash, or diagonal line). A *miss*, or an *error* (a horizontal bar), means that pins were left standing after two attempts in the frame. The small boxes in the upper right corner of each game frame are reserved for recording the results of the deliveries in each single frame, such as first- and second-ball pin counts, marks, misses, *splits* (pins other than the headpin left standing with pins missing in between—designated by an open circle) and split *conversions* (spared split—designated by an open circle with a slash through it); the large area is reserved for entering the cumulative score.

A *strike* earns 10 pins for the frame in which it was bowled *plus* the pinfall from the **next two deliveries**. A *spare* earns 10 pins for the frame in which it was bowled plus the pinfall from the **next single delivery**. To score a strike or spare, place the appropriate symbol in the small box for the frame. Then you must wait until the next frame to add the cumulative score. Any frame without a strike or spare earns only the actual pinfall for the frame, and all score entries are made current through that frame.

Scorekeeping Exercise

To help you understand how to keep score, fill in the blank game line frames (Figure I.5) according to the directions, after you read about each frame's action.

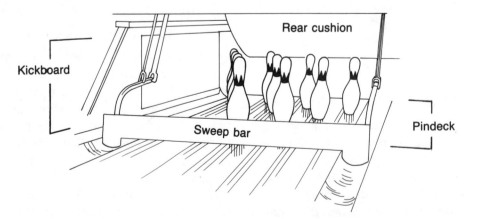

Figure I.4 The bowling lane pin area.

NAME	HDCP	1	2	3	4	5	6	7	8	9	10

Figure I.5 A blank game line.

Frames 1, 2, and 3:

You strike in your 1st, 2nd, and 3rd frames.

Score:

Mark the symbol for a strike in each of the first three frames. Write your score in the 1st frame; do not enter a score in the 2nd frame or 3rd frame yet.

Frame 4:

Next you knock down 5 pins on your first ball (delivery) of the 4th frame and only 3 pins with your second ball.

Score:

Write your score in all appropriate frames. (Hint: There should be numbers in the first four frames.)

Frame 5:

You knock down 7 pins with your first ball, leaving a split (i.e., 2 pins on one side of the lane and 1 pin on the other). You then knock down all the pins of the split, making your attempt a spare.

Score:

Make all appropriate entries in the 5th frame. Do not forget to put the symbol for a spared split in the appropriate box. Wait until the first ball of the next frame to enter a numerical score.

Frame 6:

You strike.

Score:

Write your score in the 5th frame. Mark the symbol for a strike in the 6th frame, but do not insert a numerical score yet. (The term for this designation is "a strike up.")

Frame 7, 1st ball:

You foul, getting zero for the ball, as if you had rolled it into the channel.

Score:

Wait until your spare attempt before recording any score in the 6th frame, because your strike in the 6th frame allows you to count the next *two* deliveries toward the score in the 6th frame.

Frame 7, 2nd ball:

You knock down only 9 pins on your spare attempt, which was shot at a full rack of pins.

Score:

Write your cumulative scores in the 6th and 7th frames.

Frame 8:

You knock down 8 pins on the first ball of the 8th frame, then convert the spare.

Score:

Make the appropriate entry in the 8th frame. (Hint: Because it contains a mark, there should be no numerical score in the 8th frame.)

Frame 9:

You then leave 2 pins standing on your first ball of the 9th frame, adding 8 pins to the spare in the 8th frame. However, you miss both pins on your spare attempt.

Score:

Write in your scores in the 8th and the 9th frames.

Frame 10:

You now strike on your first ball, allowing you to count the pinfall on it and the next two attempts. You strike again in the "11th," then get 7 pins on your 12th attempt.

Score:

Make all appropriate entries through the 10th frame and check your score against the correctly scored game (Figure I.6). If the scores do not match, retrace this commentary and see where your error occurred.

NAME HDCP	1	2	3	4	5	6	7	8	9	10
Sue	⊠ 30	⊠ 55	⊠ 73	5│3 81	7│∅ 101	⊠ 120	F│9 129	8│╱ 147	8│− 155	⊠⊠│7 182

Figure I.6 A correctly scored sample game.

Success Goal = Correctly match your scores with the correctly scored game

Your Score = (#) _____ correct frames

Check your scores with the correctly scored sample game. Correct your entries if necessary.

HANDICAP

In order to allow persons of unequal ability to compete with each other, a handicap is often added to the *raw*, or scratch, score of the bowler with less skill (lower average). Adding handicaps is an attempt to equalize the winning chances of all bowlers in the field.

There are many ways to determine a handicap for a bowler; none are particularly valid or reliable. However, there are two popular methods. When handicapping with the *percentage difference* method, you subtract bowler B's score from bowler C's score, and 70, 80, or 90 percent of the difference between the scores of two bowlers (or teams) represents the handicap. With the *percentage from base score* method, you assume some arbitrary *base score*—such as 200, 210, or 220. Then each bowler's average score is subtracted from the base score to get a handicap.

BOWLING TODAY

The disappearance of smaller neighborhood bowling centers devoted primarily to bowling, along with the appearance of large leisure-time complexes in which bowling is only one of the many recreational offerings, has further strengthened bowling's recreational position. However, organized play is the predominant way in which Americans engage in bowling.

Many options for organized competition are available. Adults may compete in ABC- and WIBC-sanctioned or unsanctioned leagues and tournaments. Many short handicap and scratch tournament events are conducted in major cities on almost every weekend. Youngsters may compete for fun and recognition in YABA-sanctioned leagues and tournaments, and collegiate bowlers can compete within their collegiate systems. All amateur bowlers may compete for places on the United States' international teams. Finally, opportunities exist for skilled bowlers to compete for cash prizes in events sanctioned by the PBA, the LPBT, and similar professional organizations.

Bowling fulfills the conception of ''a sport'' held by the recreational bowler because it is a pastime, a form of amusement; the activity, the social interaction, and keeping score are all ''fun.'' Even to the serious bowler or the professional aspirant, bowling can be fun because pursuing excellence is also a form of amusement.

Although mastery of bowling requires great patience and application, it is stimulating for the professional bowler because it provides an opportunity to learn new skills, to talk frequently with persons of similar interests, and to earn the admiration of others. Even practice becomes fun for the serious bowler if it is perceived as such! You will understand this point better after you have progressed through your Steps to Success.

Bowling is a worthwhile lifetime activity in terms of the moderate exercise that it provides persons of all ages. Persons of average strength and agility can compete for prizes and recognition in this sport because it is less demanding than, say, tennis, baseball, or football. Because bowling centers are typically located only a short distance from residential areas, bowling activity is also a convenient way for many persons to have a viable social life. Also, bowling can be an effective way to make friends when traveling or relocating to a new area of the country.

Organizations to contact for additional information:

American Bowling Congress (ABC)
5301 South 76th Street
Greendale, WI 53129

Ladies' Professional Bowlers Tour (LPBT)
7171 Cherryville Blvd.
Rockford, IL 61112

Professional Bowlers Association (PBA)
P.O. Box 5118
1720 Merriman Road
Akron, OH 44313

Women's International Bowling Congress
  (WIBC)
5301 South 76th Street
Greendale, WI 53129

Young American Bowling Alliance (YABA)
5301 South 76th Street
Greendale, WI 53129

Selecting Your Equipment

The two factors that determine your ability to maintain an effective grip on the bowling ball are ball *fit* (the size, location, and orientation of the holes in the ball) and the ball's total *weight*. If the ball fit is inappropriate or if the ball is too heavy, you will feel it necessary to squeeze rather than simply hold the ball, creating too tense a grip and forearm stress. Excessive tension in the forearm triggers excessive tension in the upper arm. This chain of tension destroys the desired free pendulum characteristic of the swing preceding your rolling the ball.

HOW THE BALL SHOULD FIT

There are three common ball fit styles, which are also called *grips*. They are designed to allow gripping the ball with the thumb and portions of the middle and ring fingers. Beginners like the *conventional* grip (see Figure E.1). Advanced bowlers usually progress to the wider *semifingertip* grip (see Figure E.2), or to the *fingertip* grip (see Figure E.3). Occasionally, one sees a person bowling with the thumb halfway or entirely out of the ball, imparting rapid spin with only the middle and ring fingers. Any technique that does not use the whole thumb to grip the ball, however, does not promote the free-pendulum swing and is not recommended.

The conventional fit allows you to insert your thumb to its base, and your fingers to their second joints. The *span* (the distance between the near edges of the thumbhole and a fingerhole) is proper if the crease of your finger's second joint extends 1/4 inch to 3/8 inch beyond the near edge of its fingerhole, depending on the size of your hand. This fit is the one most commonly found in *house balls* (those provided by the bowling establishment). It is recommended for beginners and persons with weaker hands because it provides a firmer finger hold.

The semifingertip fit allows you to insert your thumb to its base, and your fingers midway between their first and second joints. The

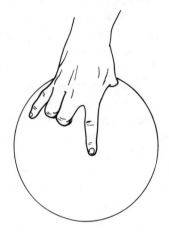

Figure E.1 Conventional fit.

Figure E.2 Semifingertip fit.

Figure E.3 Fingertip fit.

span is often judged to be proper if the near edge of the fingerhole contacts your finger anywhere between the creases of its first and second joints. The semifingertip fit does not promote a free-pendulum swing and, due to this, is not recommended for either beginners or advanced bowlers.

The fingertip fit allows you to insert your thumb to its base and your fingers to their first joints. The span is assumed to be proper if the near edge of the fingerhole lies slightly closer to the tip of your finger than midway between the creases of its first and second joints. This fit places many demands on the bowler and should be used only by advanced bowlers, with fitting of this grip done only at qualified pro shops.

Note: If you are a beginner and happen to find either a semifingertip or fingertip grip on a house ball, do not use it.

SELECTING A HOUSE BALL

The bowling establishment provides house balls for bowlers who do not own their own balls. These are available in weights from 6 to 16 pounds, and the management of the establishment attempts to keep them arranged in *ball racks* in order of weight. The hole sizes and spans generally increase with increasing total ball weight.

Select the Proper Ball Fit

Proper ball fit feels more comfortable, causes less fatigue of the hand and arm, and lessens the chance of injury through pulled muscles, tendinitis, blisters, deep calluses, and so on. To see whether ball fits your hand, use the following sequence:

Thumbhole Size: First insert your thumb into the thumbhole. While pressing one side of the thumb lightly to one side of the hole, slide the thumb in and out. If the other side of the thumb barely touches its side, the thumbhole size is appropriate. If the thumbhole is too loose or too tight, try another ball.

Correctness of Span: After selecting a thumbhole that fits, select a ball with the proper span based on descriptions previously given for the conventional ball.

Select the Proper Ball Weight

The weight of the ball you use should be appropriate for your physical makeup. You cannot effectively place a ball into your swing if it is too heavy. Further, your hand will not be able to hold the ball as it is falling into the *downswing* (the ball's backward pendular motion before you roll it). The ball will appear to pull your swing shoulder down and back, resulting in a labored, jerky series of movements. On the other hand (figuratively speaking), you will often manhandle a ball that is too light, the weight of the ball being insufficient to signal you to let it swing by its own weight.

Adult male beginner bowlers often choose balls in the 14- to 16-pound range, whereas adult females often choose balls in the 10- to 14-pound range. Youngsters often choose balls ranging from 6 to 14 pounds. Use the following "Holdout Test" and "Trial Swing" sections to check for appropriateness of weight.

Holdout Test: After selecting the ball on the basis of proper fit, pick it up to test it for total weight. The general rule is to use the heaviest ball that you feel you can control. Hold it directly in front of you with both hands and your elbows locked (see Figure E.4). If you

Figure E.4 The holdout.

cannot hold the ball in this position for at least 5 seconds, it is too heavy, and you should select a lighter ball.

Trial Swing: Look all around you and give yourself plenty of clearance. If the ball seems to be of an acceptable weight from the holdout test and passes the criteria of proper fit, as explained previously, take a short trial swing. Remember that a ball exerts more downward force at the bottom of the swing, so allow for this centrifugal "weight" when selecting your ball. Be persistent: Do not settle for a ball that seems too heavy (see Figure E.5).

Ball heaviest here

Figure E.5   The trial swing.

Problems With House Balls

Most house ball spans are the same for both the middle and the ring fingers; this allows both right- and left-handed bowlers to use house balls with equal opportunity. Unfortunately, the normal hand usually does not require equal spans—a fact that makes most house balls unsuitable for use by higher interest bowlers. The middle-finger span is too wide if the ring-finger span is correct; the ring-finger span is too narrow if the middle-finger span is correct. Also, if the ball is selected on the basis of correct thumb fit, the fingerholes are usually oversized.

Another problem exists with weight imbalances in house balls. There is a heavy spot, a *weight block*, placed in undrilled balls to compensate for the removal of ball material by drilling the holes. Often a substantial amount of this *topweight* is left in the drilled ball.

In lighter balls this remaining weight may represent a significant portion of the total weight of the ball. If such a ball is rolled slowly, it may veer off in the direction of the side of the ball in which the topweight is located. A novice bowler using such a ball may be confused and assume that this odd ball reaction resulted from poor technique; this confusion can impede progress.

If you select a ball that exhibits this veering pattern, ask a trained person to assist you in finding another. Fortunately, major manufacturers have recognized this problem and now offer light balls with very little topweight before drilling.

GRIPPING AIDS

Often your hands may be too wet or too dry to grip the ball effectively. Just as in other sports, there are various gripping aids in bowling. One is a small, porous bag containing rosin powder, which can help you attain a better grip. Another is a rosin cream. Both the powder and the cream build up on your hands and should be washed off or removed with rubbing alcohol. These substances also build up in the holes of your ball, so you are advised to use them sparingly and only if absolutely necessary.

CLOTHING

In order to ensure freedom of movement during the bowling delivery, you must be careful in your choice of clothes for bowling.

Slacks: If you are short-waisted, avoid long-waisted slacks; these will slide down, inhibiting movement of your upper legs. If your pants legs are too tight, you will not be able to bend your knees as deeply as necessary for good shotmaking, which becomes most apparent in your last step and slide. Also avoid blue jeans (which feature tight legs and heavy, irritating inseams) and shorts (they ride up, and the bottoms bind your legs at midthigh).

Shirt or Blouse: Avoid shirts and blouses with a continuous seam up the side and into the sleeve. Try to wear knit shirts or blouses, which allow free range of motion for your swing. Raglan sleeves are also desirable. A tight shirt keeps your shoulders from being held high and back, the preferred orientation. Also avoid sweaters (too bulky, they make your swing move away from your body) and long-sleeved shirts (which bind your elbows). Do not tuck your shirt or blouse too tightly into your slacks or skirt.

Especially for Women: If possible avoid wearing panty hose—especially tight hose that keep you from bending your legs sufficiently during your last step and slide. The added tension at the knee gives you a silent signal to keep your legs too straight. Also avoid full skirts (which make your swing move away from your body) and tight skirts (which bind your thighs).

Distracting Items: Other items that are sufficiently distracting to interfere with proper technique are keychains, scabbards, and electronic pagers attached to the belt; towels in the pockets; hats, caps, and unrestrained long hair; and loose eyeglasses.

THE CUSTOMIZED BALL

If you increase the frequency of your bowling to more than a couple of times per month and want to become a better bowler, you must have a better ball fit and good footing. Plan a visit to a good *pro shop* to purchase your own ball and shoes. Ask several of the best bowlers in your area for the name of a careful and skillful ball driller. Here are some helpful considerations:

- Try to buy ball, bag, and shoes together, if possible, because your shoes are an important element in providing stability for good *leverage* (lift that causes rotation) to be imparted to the ball. Furthermore, a bowler serious enough to own a ball should not have to continually dole out

money for rented shoes. The necessity for a bag is also obvious, since other accessories are usually carried in it.

- Do not immerse your hands in water (such as a bath or shower) for at least 2 hours before you have your ball fitted. If you do, there is a possibility that the grip holes will be fitted too large.

- Exercise your hand before having the ball fitted. This will stretch your grip to give a more accurate span measurement.

- Tell the pro shop operator if your hands are in common contact with slippery or drying solvents or if you have any problems, such as arthritis, that lessen your ability to grip. These factors may necessitate modifications in the fit and the ball weight.

- Tell the pro shop operator what you can afford to spend as well as where you usually bowl. Such information will have a bearing on the price and type of ball most appropriate for you.

AN ALTERNATIVE: A USED BOWLING BALL

A used bowling ball can be a good buy because it is cheaper than a new one. There are plenty of used bowling balls available. Many pro shops offer used balls, and members of the PBA and LPBT have good-quality used balls for sale. Teammates often trade balls. All these are sources of better quality used balls. Pawn shops and garage sales often sell used balls, too, but be cautious—many balls found in these places prove to be damaged due to improper storage.

If you are considering buying a used ball, check the cover for deep cracks or abrasions. Check to see whether the cover of the ball is solidly bonded to the core. If the ball has a badly damaged cover or if the ball sounds nonuniform or hollow when you tap it with a blunt object, you should probably pass it up. If you do find an acceptable used ball, take it to a pro shop for the appropriate fit. In most cases, the driller will have to *plug* and *redrill* all of the holes with your own customized grip.

GRIPPING AIDS IN YOUR BALL

You may have *finger inserts* installed in your customized ball. These gripping aids, made of plastic, help you grip your ball and impart more lift with your fingers at the release with less effort. These grips also reduce the size of the holes. Cork or rubber gripping pads are available with adhesive backing, thus making them suitable for sticking inside the holes on the gripping surfaces.

Another way of adjusting the size of a gripping hole is to place several layers of plastic tape in the back side of the hole, opposite the gripping surface. This will take up space without increasing friction like cork and rubber grips would.

SELECTING HOUSE RENTAL SHOES

In all sports, a stable *base of support* for your body is vital. Tennis players are taught to stay low and stretch out, golfers dig in when addressing the ball, and baseball players must keep their knees flexed so that they can make turns quickly. All of these actions require good footing, so special shoes are used to enhance stability through greater traction. Bowling shoes are designed to give you a stable base of support to maintain balance during your *approach* (your movements from the setup through the release of the ball) and to promote good leverage during the release.

Ask the control counter supervisor for house shoes one-half size smaller than your street shoes. If you are obtaining shoes for someone else, be sure to designate whether they are for a man or a woman, because shoes of similar numerical designation differ in size between the sexes. Remember to return your house shoes to the control counter when you are finished bowling.

PERSONAL COMMERCIAL BOWLING SHOES

In order to accommodate both right- and left-handed bowlers, house shoes have leather on both soles (see Figure E.6). This compromise is unfortunate to good bowling form and

results in less stability in the delivery. Therefore, it is recommended that you purchase your own bowling shoes.

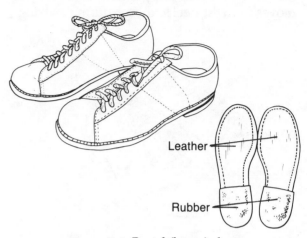

Figure E.6 Rental (house) shoes.

Good quality commercial bowling shoes allow a skid-free and stick-free heel-toe walk to the foul line; a stable anchoring of your *propelling* (nonsliding, or pushing) foot (erroneously called the *braking foot*) in preparation for the slide; and a smooth, continuous sliding motion of the *sliding* foot toward the foul line.

Make sure that your bowling shoes fit properly. Naturally, you will not buy shoes that are too short or narrow, but also avoid shoes that are too large. Such shoes allow your foot to slide inside, causing instability. A padded arch can be helpful in preventing unnecessary internal movement. The lace-to-toe models can be adjusted to accommodate the width of the foot, so this style is recommended.

Your shoes should not tire your feet. The soles should be rather thick, keeping the ball of your foot from flexing too much. If possible, the shoe should have a steel shank to keep your arch from stretching too much.

Your sliding sole should allow a free slide; it should be made of leather. In addition, your pushing sole (on your propelling foot) should allow sufficient traction to allow you to push your body forward into your slide. Buy only bowling shoes with a leather sliding sole and a rubber propelling sole (see Figure E.7).

Avoid the *universal sole* models, of which the soles of both shoes are made of the same composite material. Both heels should be made of rubber to prevent slippage as your weight moves from the heel to the toe during walking.

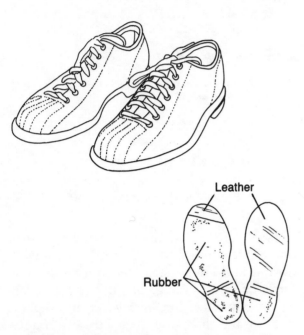

Figure E.7 Right-handed commercial bowling shoes.

PERSONAL CUSTOM-MADE BOWLING SHOES

If your feet are difficult to fit with commercial bowling shoes, you can purchase custom-made shoes. Your feet must be measured for these shoes, so you may want to locate a pro shop that will measure your feet and place the order for you. Otherwise, you may take the measurements yourself, using forms supplied by a shoe company.

CHOOSING A BOWLING BAG

You need a sturdy bag in which to carry your ball and shoes. It must be spacious enough for additional items, such as a shirt, a towel, an accessory bag, and various hand and wrist supports. You can use many different types of bags, but a bag's true tests are how well it protects your bowling balls and shoes from damage and how easy it is to carry to and from the bowling center.

Purchase the bag that is appropriate for you with respect to cost, image, and utility. If you are rough on your equipment, a molded, hard-cover type may be best for you. If you bowl only occasionally and are very fastidious with your equipment, a vinyl or Naugahyde bag may be acceptable. If you bowl many tournaments, you may prefer a canvas bag, the kind easiest to carry and store under the settee.

Consumer tip: Most bags manufactured for the purpose of carrying bowling balls are sufficiently sturdy. Other bags that resemble them may not be, so beware! It is recommended that you choose a bag that has (a) heavy or double stitching, (b) strong clasps, and (c) shoulder or handle straps that extend all the way around the bag, overlap, and are stitched to themselves.

WRIST SUPPORTS

A *technique-supportive* wrist support promotes proper form by allowing greater rotation and a quicker thumb release. All supports keep the wrist immobile during the delivery. Some supports hold the wrist straight (*extended*); some direct the hand in toward the front of the forearm (*cupped*); some direct the hand up toward the back of the forearm (*back-extended*); and some are adjustable to accomplish all three objectives (see Figure E.8).

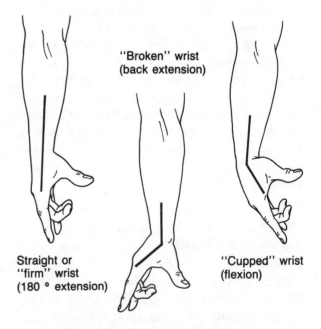

Figure E.8 Various wrist positions.

Remember, wrist supports may also hinder proper form being *technique-interfering*. They may hold your wrist in an uncomfortable position, or they may make you drop your ball before you are ready to release it. If such problems exist for you, consult a qualified pro shop operator for assistance.

THE ACCESSORY BAG

In addition to your ball, shoes, and towel, you may want to carry these other useful items in an accessory bag inside your bowling bag.

- Adhesive tape: cloth tape used to increase traction on the gripping surface inside a gripping hole

- Plastic tape: used in the back of a gripping hole to reduce its size
- Scotch Brite®: nylon webbing used to clean shoe soles and heels
- New Skin®: used to cover abrasions on the fingers and thumb
- Extra shoelaces
- Adhesive bandages

The contents of your accessory bag will change over the years as lane conditions evolve, as the frequency of your bowling changes, and as new products appear on the market.

It is recommended that, before you bowl, you warm up with moderate toning and limbering exercises. Perform your warm-up within 5 minutes of bowling so that its effects are not lost.

WARM-UP EXERCISES

Rotating Torso Stretch

Stand tall with your hands on your hips. Place your feet about 2 feet apart. Twist your upper body very slowly, first to the right and then to the left, stopping at the ends of your range of motion. Do 10 repetitions, 5 in each direction. *Caution: Do not mix planes of motion; do not bend forward or to the side while you are twisting.*

Toning Up Your Hands

Squeeze a rubber ball 10 to 20 times. If you do not have a rubber ball, alternate opening and closing your hands rapidly 30 to 40 times.

Overhead Torso Stretch

With your feet planted flatly on the floor, stretch one arm at a time as far overhead as possible. Spread the fingers of the upraised hand as wide as possible while clenching the other hand; hold this position for 5 counts. Alternate your arms, doing 5 repetitions for each arm, attempting to stretch farther each time.

Toning Up Your Arms

Hold your bowling ball directly out in front of you with both hands and with your elbows locked. Hold this position for 5 seconds. Rest for 5 seconds with your ball held at your midline. Repeat this exercise 3 times.

Quad Flex and Stretch

Slowly squat down into a sitting position while you are holding onto the ball return or the back of a chair with both hands. Concentrate to find in what position your knees are the weakest. Stay at this position, flexing and extending your knees within a range of only 6 inches. This action will limber and strengthen your quad muscle groups at their weakest range of motion. Alternate 10 up with 10 down. *Note*: *Deep knee bends are not recommended.*

Hamstring Stretch

With your back straight and your feet slightly apart and flat on the floor, stretch your arms overhead. Slowly bend forward at your waist, with knees slightly bent, until you are bent over as far as is comfortable. It is not necessary to touch your toes. Hold this position for 6 to 8 seconds and return to a standing position. Repeat this exercise 3 times.

Calf Flex and Stretch

Stand at the end of the approach with your feet slightly apart, letting your heels dangle off the end of the approach. Rise to the tiptoe position. Elevate yourself as high as you can to flex your calf muscles, then lower your heels below the level of the approach to stretch your calves. You may hold onto the ball return or a chair for stability. Alternate 10 up with 10 down.

COOL-DOWN

Usually, only strenuous sports have a cool-down. However, you should make time for some short cool-down exercises to relieve your hands, feet, hips, lower back, and legs after extended bowling activity. The cool-down routine restores flexibility and promotes circulation.

Hands

Open and close your hands slowly 20 times.

Feet

While wearing no shoes, sit down, extend your legs at the knees, and point your toes away from you. Curl your toes as far as you can without cramping. Alternate this motion with pointing your toes back toward your kneecaps. Repeat these motions 20 times, gradually building speed from slow to fast.

Lower Back

After you put on each of your street shoes, hold the bent-over, sitting position for 5 seconds to stretch your lower back.

Hips and Legs

After you put your shoes on, stand up and perform slow lunges, alternating the leading foot. Stretch back your hips; transfer your weight to the back leg by extending your front leg while keeping your upper body upright. Hold the position for a count of 5 before switching the leading foot. Repeat 3 times with each leg.

Step 1 Setup

Though the initial action in bowling is often referred to as the *stance* or the *address position*, the word *setup* is preferred because it tells you that you should systematically set yourself up in preparation for decisive movement. The setup is the preparatory phase of your approach and delivery, and it requires a ritual of checks starting with your feet and moving upward *every* time you step onto the approach.

WHY IS THE SETUP IMPORTANT?

If you were attempting to roll a hoop across a gymnasium floor at a selected target, you would not tilt the hoop before you imparted the force, but you would make sure that the hoop was perfectly in line with its intended path and perpendicular to the floor. This precaution is taken to control the movement of the hoop's *center of gravity* (the balance point—the place where the hoop's weight is centered). Swings in an object's center of gravity are represented by losses of balance in one direction, then the other, in a repeating fashion. If you did not ensure control of the hoop's motion from the start, the hoop would wobble, skid, and veer off, probably falling down short of its intended goal.

Good balance and accuracy are benefits derived from maintaining control of your own center of gravity during movement. Such control begins with a well-balanced setup. If you systematically set yourself up in proper balance—with your feet supporting your hips, your shoulders parallel to your hips, your back muscles stable, and your ball held in line with your shoulder and the intended ball path—you will be better prepared to control your center of gravity when you take your first step and push your ball into the swing.

HOW TO EXECUTE THE SETUP

To begin, carefully pick up your ball off the ball return (see Figure 1.1a) and place it in your nonbowling or *balance* hand, to avoid unnecessary tension in your bowling arm. Stand approximately 2 feet from the end of the approach and look at the set of dots closest to you. This is termed the *next-up position* (see Figure 1.1b).

From the next-up position, check for clearance of bowlers to either side of you and step up onto the approach to begin your setup ritual. Because you need a specific place to stand and to look at while you are setting up, place the inner edge of the sole of your sliding foot on the dot 5 boards to the *outside* (to your *swingside*, the side of the lane nearer your bowling arm) of the large center dot of either set of approach dots (see Figure 1.1c).

Next check to make sure that your toes and heels form a square and that the toes of both feet are pointed straight toward your target. Be sure that your knees are straight; your hips and shoulders should be parallel to each other and perpendicular to your feet. These actions are collectively termed "squaring" or "squaring up" (see Figure 1.1d). Hold your back upright and your head high—be "snooty"!

Look—in fact, stare—at the second arrow from the swingside channel during your setup. If you were making an actual delivery, you would follow this visual fixation point out of the bottoms, not the tops, of your eyes. (By the way, bifocal or trifocal glasses will interfere with your ability to keep your head up during movement.)

Mental picture: The bottoms of your eyes are emitting laser beams that are burning a hole in the second arrow!

Next put your fingers in the gripping holes and transfer your ball to a position in line with your bowling arm and the second arrow (see Figure 1.1e). Keep your forearm slightly raised up and hold most of the ball's weight in your balance arm, not your bowling arm. Focus more strongly on the second arrow, take a deep breath, exhale, and hold your stomach in (see Figure 1.1f).

Figure 1.1 Keys to Success: Setup

Preparation Phase

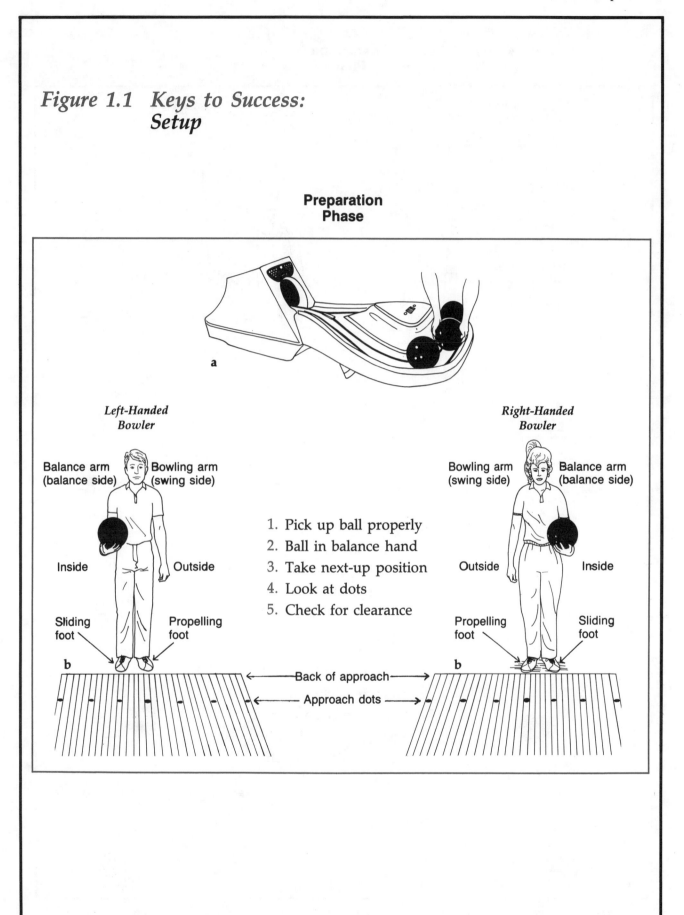

Left-Handed Bowler

Balance arm (balance side)   Bowling arm (swing side)

Inside   Outside

Sliding foot   Propelling foot

b

Right-Handed Bowler

Bowling arm (swing side)   Balance arm (balance side)

Outside   Inside

Propelling foot   Sliding foot

b

1. Pick up ball properly
2. Ball in balance hand
3. Take next-up position
4. Look at dots
5. Check for clearance

← Back of approach →
← Approach dots →

Execution Phase

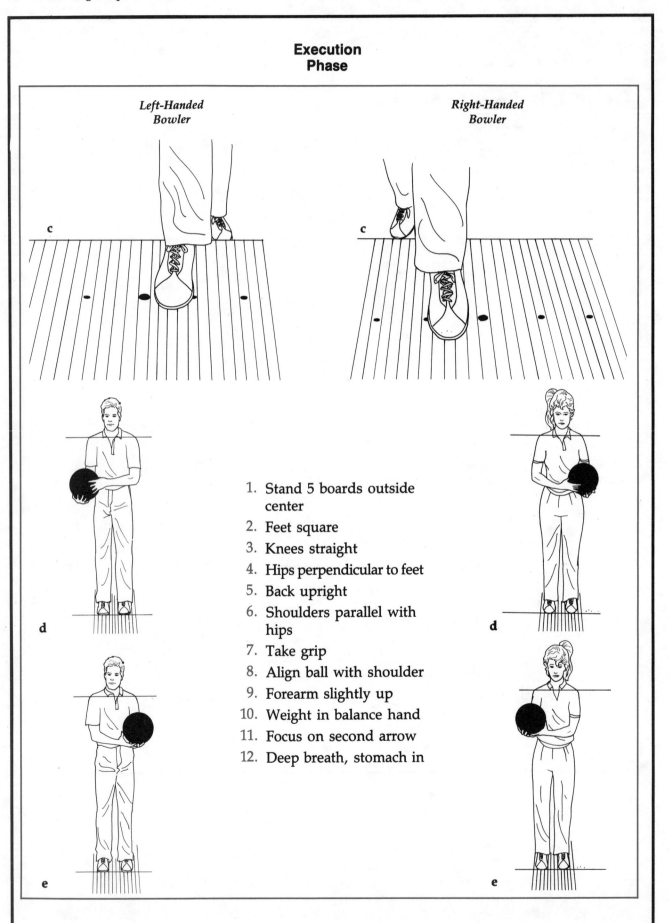

Left-Handed Bowler

Right-Handed Bowler

1. Stand 5 boards outside center
2. Feet square
3. Knees straight
4. Hips perpendicular to feet
5. Back upright
6. Shoulders parallel with hips
7. Take grip
8. Align ball with shoulder
9. Forearm slightly up
10. Weight in balance hand
11. Focus on second arrow
12. Deep breath, stomach in

Recovery
Phase

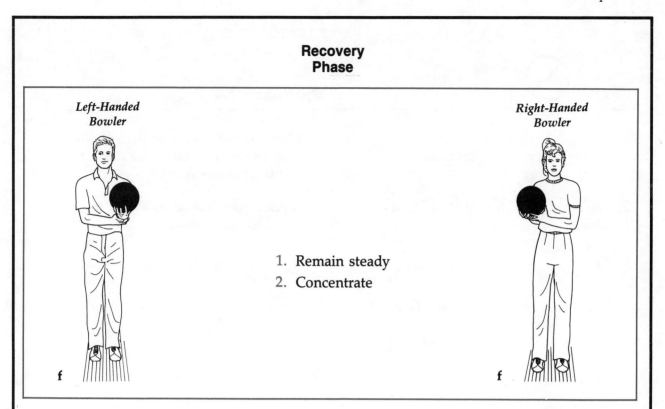

*Left-Handed
Bowler*

*Right-Handed
Bowler*

1. Remain steady
2. Concentrate

Detecting Setup Errors

A well-constructed, minimal-tension setup is essential for a well-balanced approach and delivery. However, the effects of errors in the setup may not be apparent until the ball is released, seen in either an unbalanced follow-through position or the misdirected path of the ball rolling down the lane.

You can lessen your percentage of misdirected *shots* (deliveries) if you correct setup errors before beginning any approach movement. To do this, you must learn how to recognize the difference between the correct and the incorrect setup characteristics. Then you must know how to correct the errors. Some common setup errors and suggestions on how to correct them now follow.

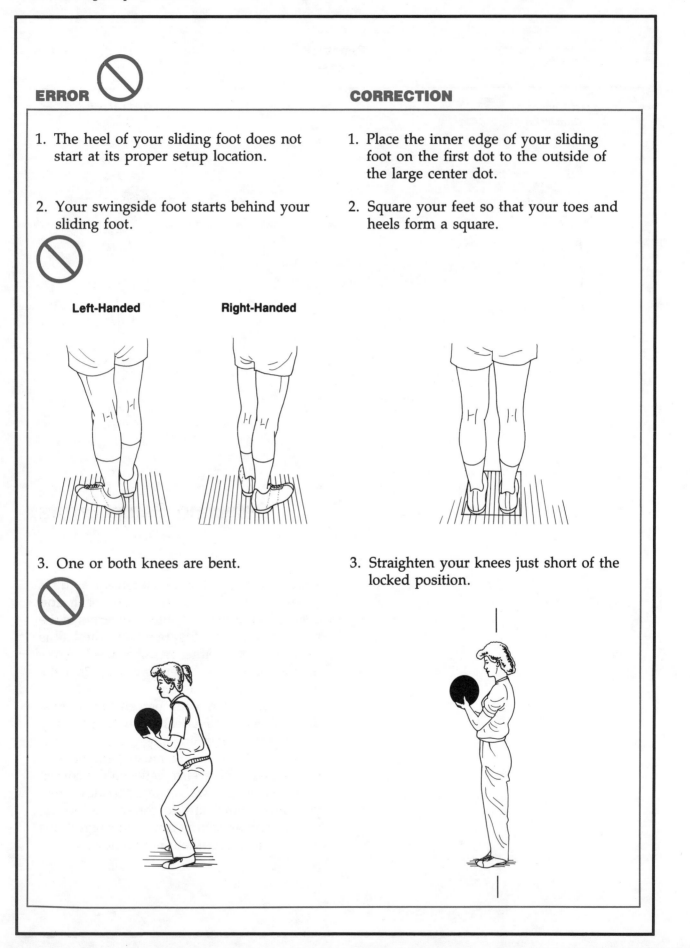

ERROR

CORRECTION

1. The heel of your sliding foot does not start at its proper setup location.

1. Place the inner edge of your sliding foot on the first dot to the outside of the large center dot.

2. Your swingside foot starts behind your sliding foot.

2. Square your feet so that your toes and heels form a square.

Left-Handed   **Right-Handed**

3. One or both knees are bent.

3. Straighten your knees just short of the locked position.

CORRECTION

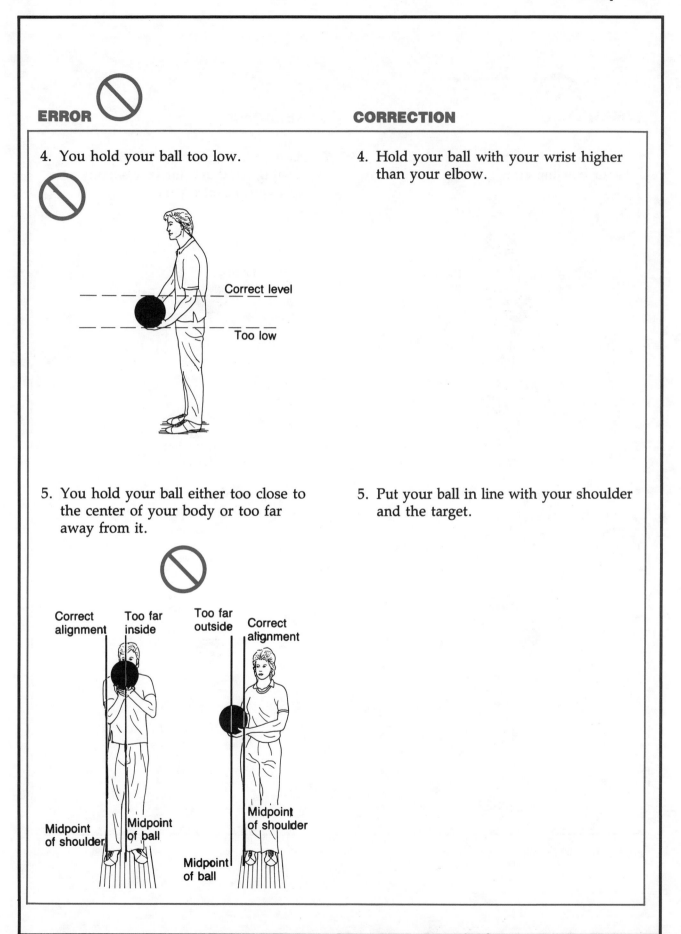

4. You hold your ball too low.

4. Hold your ball with your wrist higher than your elbow.

Correct level

Too low

5. You hold your ball either too close to the center of your body or too far away from it.

5. Put your ball in line with your shoulder and the target.

Correct alignment   Too far inside   Too far outside   Correct alignment

Midpoint of shoulder   Midpoint of ball   Midpoint of shoulder

Midpoint of ball

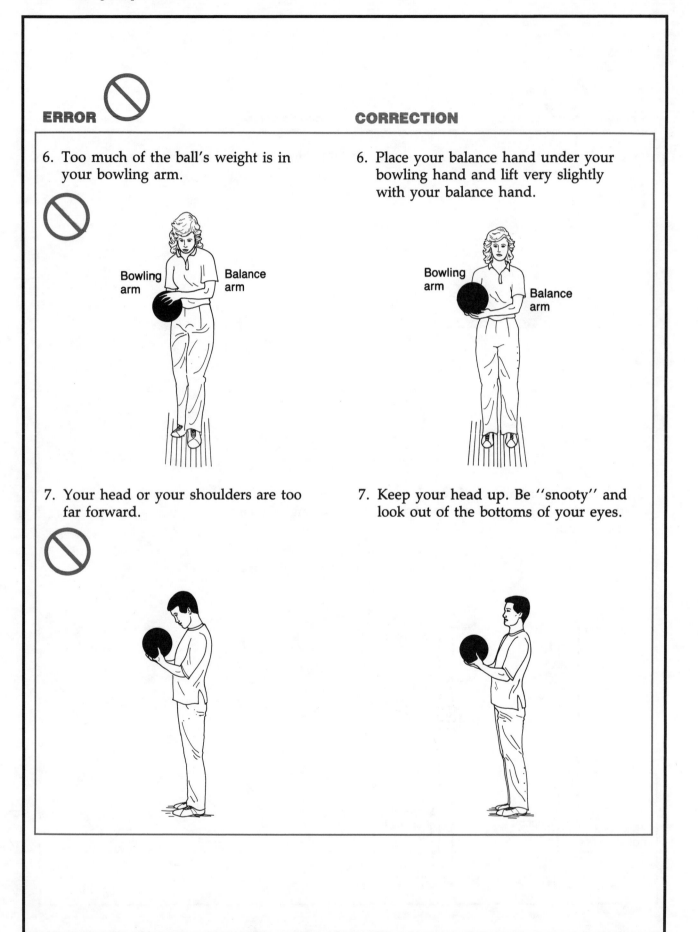

ERROR 🚫

CORRECTION

6. Too much of the ball's weight is in your bowling arm.

6. Place your balance hand under your bowling hand and lift very slightly with your balance hand.

Bowling arm   Balance arm

Bowling arm   Balance arm

7. Your head or your shoulders are too far forward.

7. Keep your head up. Be "snooty" and look out of the bottoms of your eyes.

Setup Drills

1. *Check Sequence Run-Through*

The sequence of checks leading to a proper setup position will help you learn how to execute the setup faster. Study the Setup Keys to Success in Figure 1.1 thoroughly and, when ready, use your ball and act out each Key as you recite your intentions to your partner, who will check you and compute your score. Remember to use the assigned setup location and to look at the second arrow from your swingside channel.

Success Goal = recite and perform all 19 Keys to Success in 5 or fewer attempts

Your Score =

    Attempt 1 _____

    Attempt 2 _____

    Attempt 3 _____

    Attempt 4 _____

    Attempt 5 _____

2. *Balance Awareness*

Focus your attention on the quality of your body balance.

a. From your completed setup position, lean forward slowly, paying close attention to the shifting of your weight to the balls of your feet. Lean forward just enough to feel that you are about to lose your balance. Return to the upright position. Next lean to the swingside, paying attention to weight distribution on the feet. Lean to the swingside just enough to feel your balance-side foot lift off of the approach.

b. Repeat (a), but close your eyes after assuming the completed setup position. Concentrate on the feeling of balance.

Success Goal = 20 total lean comparisons

a. With eyes open

   5 comparisons of forward leans, balance

   5 comparisons of swingside leans, balance

b. With eyes closed

   5 comparisons of forward leans, balance

   5 comparisons of swingside leans, balance

Your Score =

a. Eyes open (10 leans)

   (#) _____ comparisons of forward leans, balance

   (#) _____ comparisons of swingside leans, balance

b. Eyes closed (10 leans)

   (#) _____ comparisons of forward leans, balance

   (#) _____ comparisons of swingside leans, balance

3. Alignment Awareness

Focus your attention on how well you are aligned with the second arrow. From the completed setup position, while keeping your eyes on the second arrow, look at your swingside shoulder, then at the ball, and finally at the second arrow. Move so that the three lie along an imaginary straight line perfectly perpendicular to your shoulders.

a. Without moving your heels, point your toes 3 inches to the outside. Again check the relationship of your shoulder, your ball, and the second arrow. Note that the three are no longer aligned. Return to your correctly aligned position.

b. Point your toes 3 inches to the inside and repeat the same checks, again noting the loss of alignment and returning to the correctly aligned position.

Success Goal = 10 total comparisons

   5 comparisons of outside misalignments with correct alignments

   5 comparisons of inside misalignments with correct alignments

Your Score =

   (#) _____ comparisons of outside misalignments with correct alignments

   (#) _____ comparisons of inside misalignments with correct alignments

4. Bowling Arm Tension Awareness

Focus your attention on the amount of tension in your bowling arm in the setup position. Your ability to reduce bowling arm tension at will during your setup ritual will greatly influence your free-pendulum swing.

While in your setup position, tense your bowling hand and arm, squeezing your grip on the ball and carrying the majority of the ball's weight in your bowling arm. Alternate this action with a conscious reduction of tension in your bowling hand and arm, saying to yourself, "Looser, looser."

Mental picture: Your forearm and upper arm become less tense as you keep your wrist firm and eliminate the squeezing sensation of your fingers in the ball.

Support all of the ball's weight in your balance hand and arm, relieving the tension in your bowling arm. Simply hold your ball in the grip; do not squeeze it. Alternate 10 tense and 10 relaxed bowling arms, noting the contrast between sensations. Note also how each action affects the tension in your back and shoulders.

Tense
bowling
arm

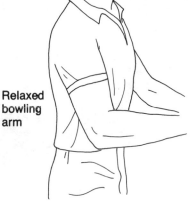
Relaxed
bowling
arm

Success Goal = 20 total actions, 10 tense biceps alternating with 10 relaxed biceps

Your Score = (#) _____ actions

Setup
Keys to Success Checklist

You must be sure that your setup is stable and well balanced. Ask your teacher, coach, or a trained observer to qualitatively evaluate your technique according to the checklist below.

Preparation
Phase

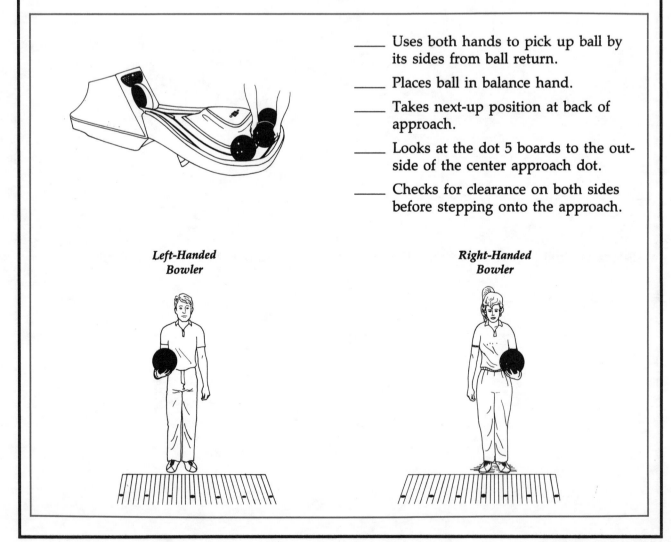

_____ Uses both hands to pick up ball by its sides from ball return.

_____ Places ball in balance hand.

_____ Takes next-up position at back of approach.

_____ Looks at the dot 5 boards to the outside of the center approach dot.

_____ Checks for clearance on both sides before stepping onto the approach.

Left-Handed Bowler

Right-Handed Bowler

Execution
Phase

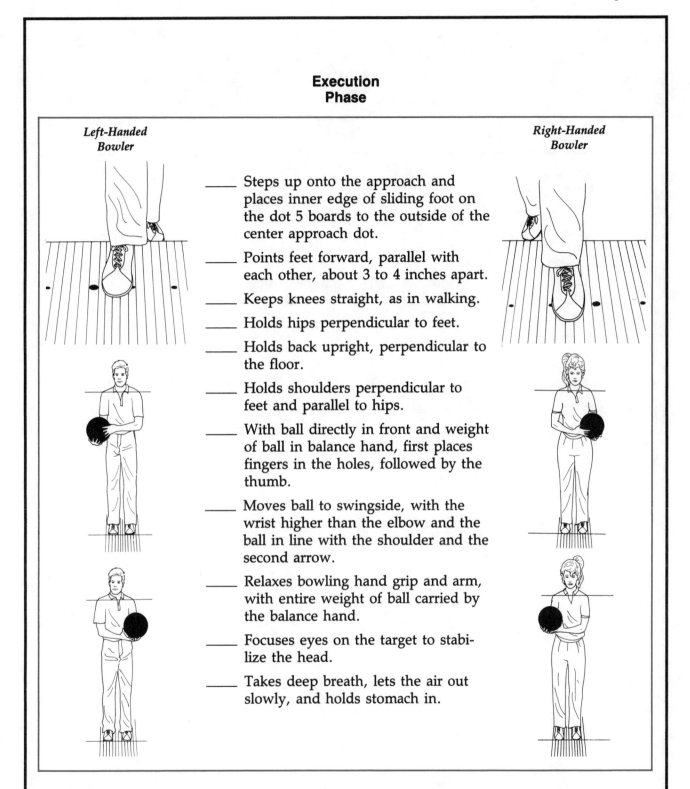

Left-Handed Bowler   *Right-Handed Bowler*

_____ Steps up onto the approach and places inner edge of sliding foot on the dot 5 boards to the outside of the center approach dot.

_____ Points feet forward, parallel with each other, about 3 to 4 inches apart.

_____ Keeps knees straight, as in walking.

_____ Holds hips perpendicular to feet.

_____ Holds back upright, perpendicular to the floor.

_____ Holds shoulders perpendicular to feet and parallel to hips.

_____ With ball directly in front and weight of ball in balance hand, first places fingers in the holes, followed by the thumb.

_____ Moves ball to swingside, with the wrist higher than the elbow and the ball in line with the shoulder and the second arrow.

_____ Relaxes bowling hand grip and arm, with entire weight of ball carried by the balance hand.

_____ Focuses eyes on the target to stabilize the head.

_____ Takes deep breath, lets the air out slowly, and holds stomach in.

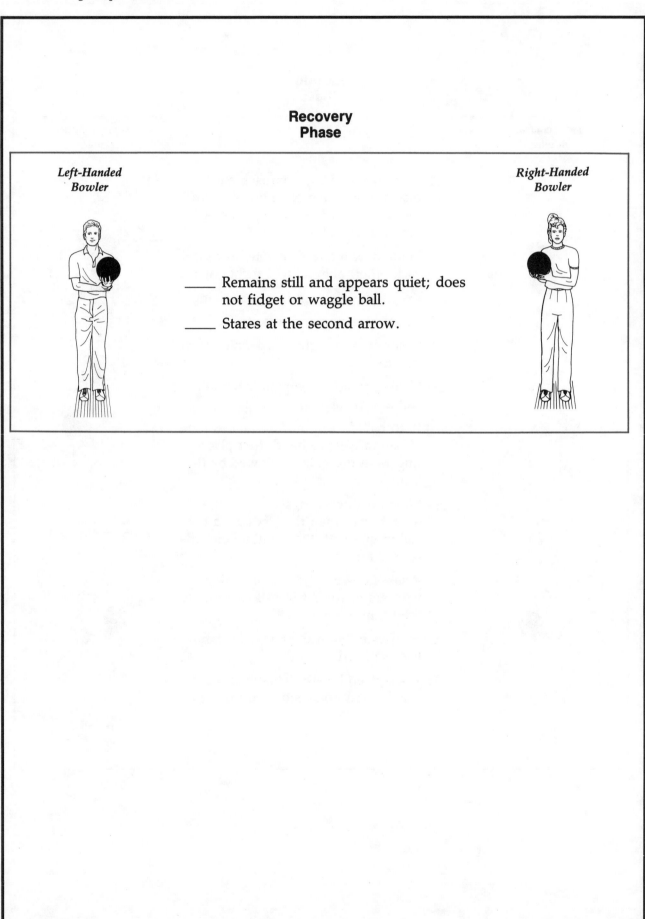

Recovery
Phase

*Left-Handed
Bowler*

*Right-Handed
Bowler*

_____ Remains still and appears quiet; does not fidget or waggle ball.

_____ Stares at the second arrow.

Step 2 **Pendulum Swing**

Just like the pendulum on a grandfather clock, your bowling arm must be a free pendulum in the approach swing. No muscular force should be used to speed up or slow down the ball. The ball must simply fall into the downswing, then back into the *forward swing*, drawn only by the force of gravity.

With a partner assisting you, and your using a modified setup position, you will learn the feel of the ideal free-pendulum swing and the feel of undesirable deviations from this ideal. Also, you will learn how to maintain support and balance while the ball is in motion.

WHY IS THE PENDULUM SWING IMPORTANT?

A musician uses a metronome to establish a consistent rhythm, or *cadence*, for a musical performance. You can use the all-important free-pendulum swing to establish a consistent cadence for your footwork.

Unfortunately, many bowlers spend a lifetime of bowling trying to fit their footwork patterns to swings that are neither consistent nor free. One important fact to remember is that a short arm has a short-timed pendulum swing; the ball will take less time to move through the arc of the swing than that of a person with a longer arm. Hence, the footwork may be taken more quickly. The longer arm

and the resulting longer timed swing requires slower footwork.

Because a person's free-pendulum swing always takes the same amount of time—from the extended pushaway through the downswing, backswing, and forward swing to the release—it is possible to fit the pace of your footwork to this very reliable timing element. If you always allow your ball to swing as an unforced or uninhibited pendulum, you have one consistent element around which to build your entire approach and delivery.

HOW TO EXECUTE A PENDULUM SWING

With the pendulum swing, you simply allow gravity to draw the ball down, up, and back; you neither pull it down nor keep it from falling. Your elbow should be locked, your wrist should be straight and firm, and your shoulder should act as a *pivot*, or centerpoint, for the swing.

Figure 2.1 shows the timing for the pendulum swing. Your ball should be straight out in front of you on the count of "one." It should be passing your swingside leg on the count of "two." On "three" the ball should reach the top of your backswing. Lastly, on "four" your ball should be passing your swingside leg during the forward swing (see Figure 2.2).

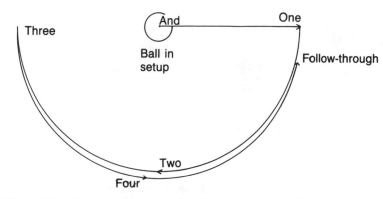

Figure 2.1 Timing of the swing in a four-step approach.

Figure 2.2 Keys to Success:
Pendulum Swing

**Preparation
Phase**

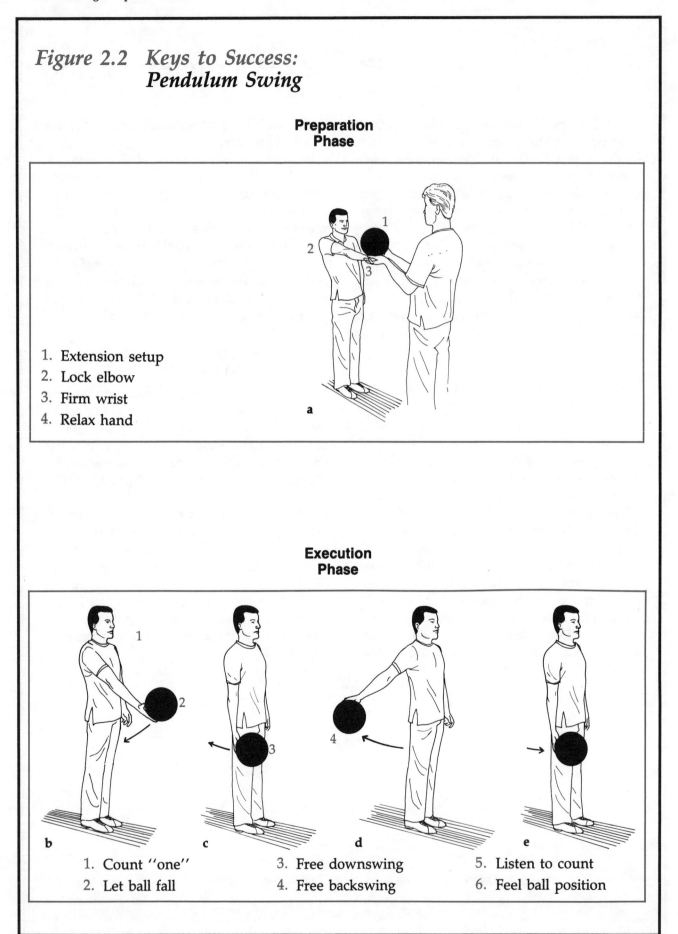

1. Extension setup
2. Lock elbow
3. Firm wrist
4. Relax hand

a

**Execution
Phase**

b   c   d   e

1. Count "one"   3. Free downswing   5. Listen to count
2. Let ball fall   4. Free backswing   6. Feel ball position

**Recovery
Phase**

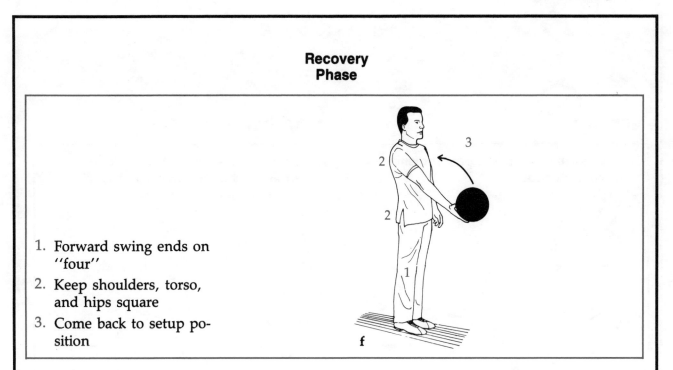

1. Forward swing ends on "four"
2. Keep shoulders, torso, and hips square
3. Come back to setup position

Detecting Pendulum Swing Errors

A properly-directed free-pendulum swing appears to be relatively effortless. However, to the untrained eye, even a retarded, a hurried, or a misaligned swing may appear to be correct; of course, such characteristics are undesirable. They are most apparent at the release, with the ball being late with respect to the feet, and at the follow-through, which incorrectly either crosses the body or is directed to the outside, away from the body.

You can increase your consistency through a properly aligned free-pendulum swing if you learn how to recognize the differences between the correct and incorrect pendulum-swing characteristics and know how to correct them. Some common pendulum swing errors and suggestions on how to correct them follow.

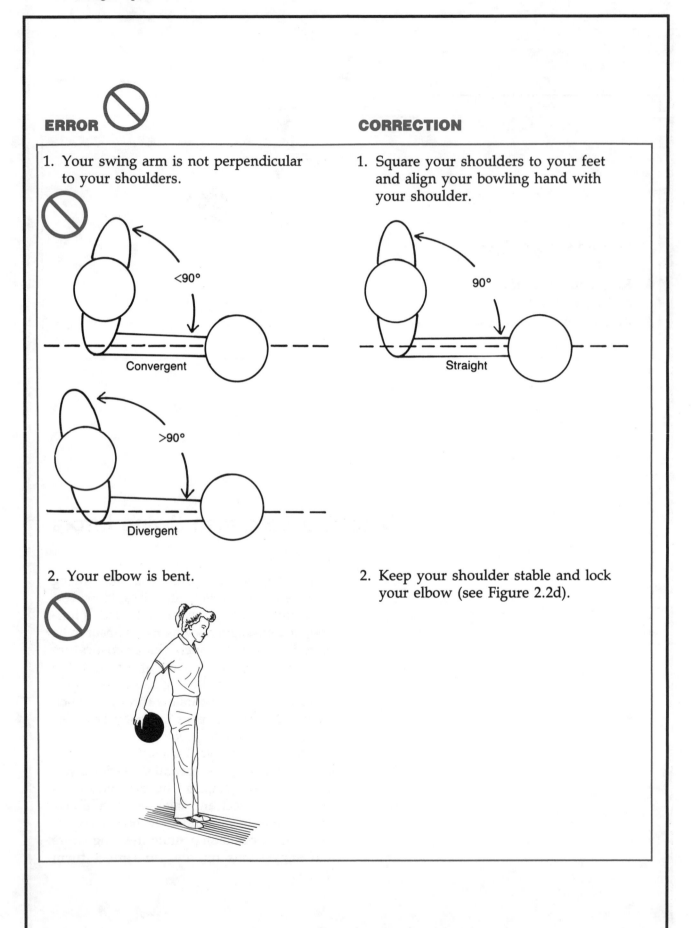

ERROR

CORRECTION

1. Your swing arm is not perpendicular to your shoulders.

1. Square your shoulders to your feet and align your bowling hand with your shoulder.

<90°

Convergent

90°

Straight

>90°

Divergent

2. Your elbow is bent.

2. Keep your shoulder stable and lock your elbow (see Figure 2.2d).

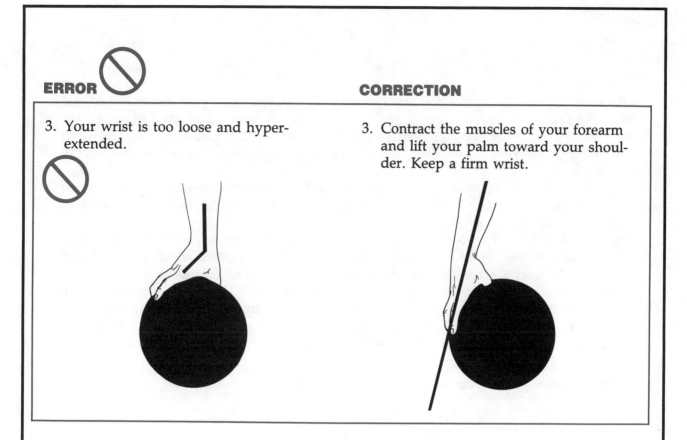

ERROR ⊘   **CORRECTION**

3. Your wrist is too loose and hyper-extended.

3. Contract the muscles of your forearm and lift your palm toward your shoulder. Keep a firm wrist.

Pendulum Swing Drills

Safety Tips: All of the following drills will be performed with you and your practice partner face-to-face. Your partner will be starting and stopping your swing. Swing only in line with the approach—never at an angle to it. Always check behind you before swinging a ball. Warn your partner to keep face and hands clear of your swing. Be sure that he or she stops your swing with the hands only on the sides of the ball.

1. Free Swing Cadence

With your partner standing on the approach, face-to-face with you and approximately 3 feet away, assume your normal setup position. Modify your setup by extending your ball out, directly in line with your shoulder. Keeping your grip on the ball and with your palm up, place the ball into your partner's hands and drop your balance arm to your side. This is called the *extension setup* position, and it will be used in drills for this and some of the subsequent steps.

   Let your partner hold the weight of the ball by placing the palms of his or her hands on either side of the ball. Your partner should prepare you by saying, "Let me have all of the weight of your ball . . . more . . . more." When he or she feels that you have given up most of the weight of the ball and if you are squared to him or her, with your elbow locked and your wrist firm, your partner should say, ''When you are ready, close your eyes and say one.'' Tense the muscles of your spine in preparation for the ball to fall. When you feel ready to allow the ball to swing, say ''one.'' Upon hearing this, your partner will let the ball fall into the swing.

Note: If you tend to lose your grip on the ball as it starts into the downswing, it may be improperly fitted, too heavy, or both. In this case, have your ball checked by a trained person, and replace it if necessary.

Simply follow the ball's arc with your arm. Focus on the stability of your body and of your shoulder joint. Do not retard or accelerate the swing. Either is termed *muscling the ball*, and must be avoided, or the consistency of the total swing time will disappear.

When the ball passes your swingside leg, your partner should say ''two''; when the ball reaches the top of your backswing, your partner should say ''three''; and when the ball again passes the swingside leg on the forward swing, your partner should say ''four.'' Your partner's count indicates the cadence established by your swing, so remember it well!

Success Goal = 10 consecutive free-pendulum swings

Your Score = (#) _____ swings

2. *Muscling Awareness*

Repeat the first drill with the following modifications. Your objective is to modify your swing speed through muscular force in an attempt to understand the feel of muscling the ball.

a. *Feeling a retarded swing.* Just before telling your partner that you are ready, deliberately tense your arm by lifting a little of the weight of the ball slightly up while it is still in your partner's hands. Let your partner know what you are doing. Then close your eyes and say ''one,'' whereupon your partner releases the ball. Keep your arm in this slightly tense state during the entire swing. Focus your attention on the tension in your arm and notice that your swing seems slower than the free swing.

Note the speed of your swing while your partner counts, ''two, three, four,'' as the ball passes through the positions indicated in the previous drill. Do this drill nine times, lifting more of the ball's weight out of your partner's hands each time, until you have lifted the ball completely off your partner's hands before you start your swing. Score yourself, indicating the differences in swing speed as you felt it. Slow = S, Slower = 2S, and so on.

Success Goal = 9 repetitions (3 with each level of lifting weight)

Your Score =

a. with some weight of ball, swing speed is

_____ (attempt 1)

_____ (attempt 2)

_____ (attempt 3)

b. with more ball weight, swing speed is

_____ (attempt 1)

_____ (attempt 2)

_____ (attempt 3)

c. with most of the ball's weight, swing speed is

_____ (attempt 1)

_____ (attempt 2)

_____ (attempt 3)

b. *Feeling an accelerated swing.* Just before signaling your partner that you are ready, deliberately pull the ball down slightly while it is still in your partner's hands. Let your partner know what you are doing. Then close your eyes and say, "one." Keep your arm in this tense state during the swing. Focus your attention on the tension in your arm and notice that the swing seems faster than the free swing.

Note the speed of the swing while your partner counts, "two, three, four," as the ball passes the positions indicated in the above drill. Accomplish this drill nine times, pulling down more each time, adding slightly to the ball's weight in your partner's hands before you start your swing. Score yourself below, indicating the differences in swing speed as you felt it. Fast = F, Faster = 2F, and so on.

Success Goal = 9 repetitions (3 with each level of pulling weight)

Your Score =

a. with some weight of ball, swing speed is

_____ (attempt 1)

_____ (attempt 2)

_____ (attempt 3)

b. with more ball weight, swing speed is

_____ (attempt 1)

_____ (attempt 2)

_____ (attempt 3)

c. with most of the ball's weight, swing speed is

_____ (attempt 1)

_____ (attempt 2)

_____ (attempt 3)

3. Hoist and Clip Awareness

In this drill you will practice two errors so that you can feel the difference between them and a pendulum swing, recognize the tendency to make these errors, and correct them. Neither error is as distinct in the drill as when you take a full approach.

a. *Feeling a hoist.* A *hoist* is the act of pulling the ball up into the backswing with the muscles of the back of the arm, the shoulder, and the back; it is not a free swing. A hoist is usually caused by a low, late pushaway (discussed in Step 10) and a retarded swing—the most common causes of late ball timing.

   Have your partner hold your ball 2 feet lower than the usual extension setup position. This should place the ball at a level between your waist and knees. Do not lean over; remain erect. When you signal to begin the swing by saying "one," let the ball swing freely. Focus your attention on your tendency to hoist or lift the ball up behind you. Have your partner complete the count as in the previous drill. Alternate the hoist 3 times with a free-pendulum swing to compare the difference.

b. *Feeling a clip.* A *clip* is the act of stopping the backswing short with the muscles of the shoulder and upper arm before it reaches the top of the backswing. A clip may be caused by a high or early pushaway, or limited flexibility of the shoulder. The most common result is that the swing is early in relation to the steps—ahead of the footwork.

   Have your partner hold your ball 1 foot higher than the usual extension setup position, putting the ball at a level above the level of your shoulders. Remain erect. When you signal to begin the swing by saying "one," let the ball swing freely. Focus your attention on your tendency to stop the ball short in your backswing. Have your partner complete the count as in the previous drills. Alternate the clip 3 times with a free-pendulum swing to compare the difference.

Success Goals =

   a. 3 hoist and free-pendulum swing comparisons
   b. 3 clip and free-pendulum swing comparisons

Your Score =

   a. (#) _____ hoist and pendulum swing comparisons
   b. (#) _____ clip and pendulum swing comparisons

4. Swing Alignment Awareness

This drill introduces two errors in *swing plane* alignment (path of the ball in the swing), so that you can feel their effects on your body stabilization.

Bumpout swing

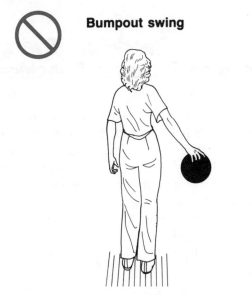

Wraparound swing

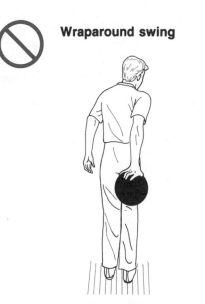

a. *Feeling a bumpout (convergent) swing.* Have your partner hold your ball 6 to 8 inches farther to the *inside* than in the ideal extension setup position. This action should place the ball almost directly in front of your body's centerline. Remain squared otherwise; do not turn your bowling shoulder inward.

  When you signal to begin the swing by saying ''one,'' let the ball swing freely. Focus your attention on the ball pulling you off balance to the back and toward your swingside. This pulling is even more distinct now than when a full approach is taken, because then one or more steps would be taken in the opposite direction to regain control of your body's center of gravity. The bumpout swing can cause you to miss your target to the inside. Alternate this error three times with properly directed swings to compare the difference.

b. *Feeling a wraparound (divergent) swing.* Have your partner hold your ball 6 to 8 inches farther to the *outside* than in the ideal extension setup position. This action should place the ball 6 to 8 inches to the outside of your ideal swing plane. Remain squared otherwise; do not turn your bowling shoulder outward.

  When you signal to begin the swing by saying ''one,'' let the ball swing freely. Focus your attention on the tendency of the ball to pull you off balance to the front and to the outside of your swing. This is even more distinct than when a full approach is taken, because one or more steps would be taken in the opposite direction to regain control of the body's center of gravity. The wraparound swing can cause you to miss your target to the outside. Alternate this error three times with a properly directed swing to compare the difference.

Success Goals =

a. 3 bumpout and free-pendulum swing comparisons

b. 3 wraparound and free-pendulum swing comparisons

Your Score =

a. (#) _____ bumpout and pendulum swing comparisons

b. (#) _____ wraparound and pendulum swing comparisons

Pendulum Swing
Keys to Success Checklist

You have learned the feel of a relaxed pendulum swing. It is important that your arm is sufficiently relaxed while your back and shoulders are held stable. Gravity must do the work of moving the ball through the swing. To check for these characteristics, ask your teacher, coach, or a trained observer to qualitatively evaluate your technique according to the checklist below.

**Preparation
Phase**

_____ Assumes extension setup position, extending bowling arm.

_____ Locks elbow and keeps grip on ball.

_____ Keeps firm wrist without squeezing grip on ball.

_____ Gives entire weight of ball to partner.

Execution
Phase

____ Closes eyes and gives the signal "one" for partner to let ball fall into pendulum swing.

____ Allows ball to swing down and up to top of backswing.

____ Uses free downswing; does not slow down or speed up ball.

____ Uses free forward swing.

____ Listens as partner calls, "Two, three, four," and notes position of ball on each count.

____ Feels position of ball with respect to each count.

Recovery
Phase

____ Ends free forward swing as ball stops on the count of "four."

____ Keeps shoulders, torso, and hips square as in setup.

____ Either comes back to setup position to catch ball's momentum or partner catches on both sides of ball.

Step 3 **Footwork**

Proper footwork consists of heel-toe steps identical to the way you normally walk. Also, footwork should be in time with the free-pendulum swing. Proper footwork is properly timed, provides good balance, and promotes a strong finish. Heel-toe steps are preferred to shuffling steps because they are similar to a normal walking pattern and because touching the heel down at the exact instant of a count promotes consistent timing. You are cautioned not to use shuffling steps because they are more difficult to keep in time and they promote premature bending of the legs.

One point should be emphasized with respect to timing: you must fit your footwork to your swing—not the other way around. The best way for you to make this important link is to learn your steps in accordance with the cadence with which you are already familiar; however, you will first learn footwork without swinging the ball.

WHY IS FOOTWORK IMPORTANT?

1. *Timing*. Footwork that is properly synchronized with the swing cadence is more consistent and allows the force generated by the swing to peak on each step. When outside influences begin to excite a bowler (an increase in *state anxiety*), the bowler's most common reaction is to increase the footwork pace, a condition called *fast feet*. Fast feet make the ball late with respect to the footwork, and the bowler falls victim to various problems that are discussed in depth in Step 10. Fast feet are difficult for a bowler to sense, because his or her attention is usually focused on a visual target.

2. *Balance*. Proper footwork also helps establish a stable base of support. You must have good footing to prevent loss of balance. Further, control of a heavy object (a bowling ball) is facilitated by better contact of your feet with a solid surface (the approach).

3. *Finish*. The way in which you walk to the foul line, the mechanics of your *gait*, has a great bearing upon your ability to put yourself in a high-leverage position (in which you can impart more rotation to the ball with your fingers) at the foul line. Such a superior finish position will allow you to hit your target more often and to attain more *pin action* (collisions of the pins) upon ball impact. Greater pin action results from *ball projection*, which is maximized when the fingers lift the ball up and out and onto the lane surface while the hand is on the upswing, a movement made more easily from a bent-knee and upright-back position. A relatively normal walking gait during your bowling approach will enhance your consistency in achieving a superior finish position.

HOW TO EXECUTE FOOTWORK

You will now learn the footwork unassisted by a partner. After taking your position on the approach for a normal setup position, hold your ball with both hands at your midline, waist-level and touching your body; keep the ball against your body throughout the following foot movements. Next prepare yourself for movement by beginning a cadence. This rhythm will give you a better chance of keeping your feet in time with your swing. Remember, the cadence is the element most responsible for consistent bowling performance.

After establishing your rhythm, step forward halfway between ''four'' and the next count of ''one,'' so that the heel of your swingside foot touches down on the count of ''one.'' Keep walking in a heel-toe fashion in rhythm with your cadence, holding your ball firmly at your midline.

Touch down your sliding-foot heel on ''two.'' On ''three'' touch down your swingside heel on the approach, so that it will be an anchor against which to push your balance-side (*sliding*) foot forward in the *slide* to the foul line. Immediately begin to deeply bend your swingside knee. On "four" touch down your sliding foot sole and continue to push forward, using your swingside foot as the anchor. Keep your back upright and let your hips move down as your swingside foot remains anchored and your sliding foot moves forward, increasing the distance between your feet.

Note. Do not bend your knees until the count of "three." Doing so, known as *premature bend*, would interfere with your ability to impart accurate direction and effective roll to your ball at the release. It would cause your swingside knee to be too greatly bent prior to the slide. Your body's center of gravity would thus be too low for you to position your swingside foot far enough ahead of the other foot to give you good positioning for your push; the swingside foot would be too far back. The swingside sole would be the only part of the foot in contact with the approach prior to your push. Thus, your foot would slip, coming off

the approach and into the air. Your hips (and shoulders) would turn away from the swing, thereby depriving you of valuable leverage. In order to reclaim some of the lost leverage, you would have to use excessive shoulder and arm force (muscling).

Your desired final recovery position is similar to that used by a skier landing after a distance jump or by a fencer during a lunge. This posture is termed *sitting tall*. It is described as (a) your back being upright, with no more than 20 degrees of forward lean; (b) your sliding leg being bent approximately 90 degreees, with its foot positioned under your body's center of gravity; (c) your swingside leg being extended back, almost straight, with the sole of this foot in the same place on the approach as when the slide began; and (d) your shoulders and hips being parallel to each other and perpendicular to the follow-through. Remember the term *sitting tall* and the description for this position well—it is referred to many times in this and subsequent Keys to Success (see Figure 3.1).

Figure 3.1 Keys to Success: Footwork

Preparation Phase

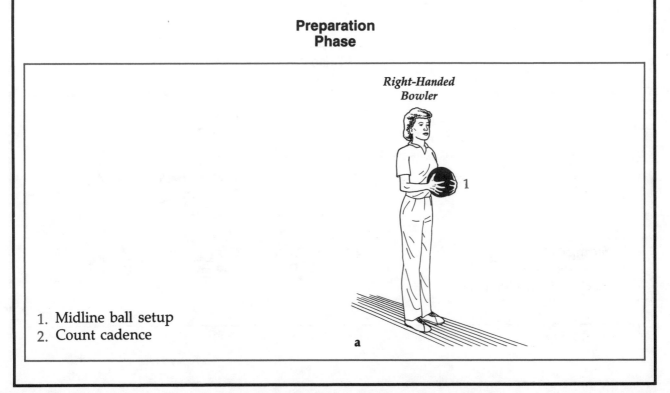

Right-Handed Bowler

1. Midline ball setup
2. Count cadence

a

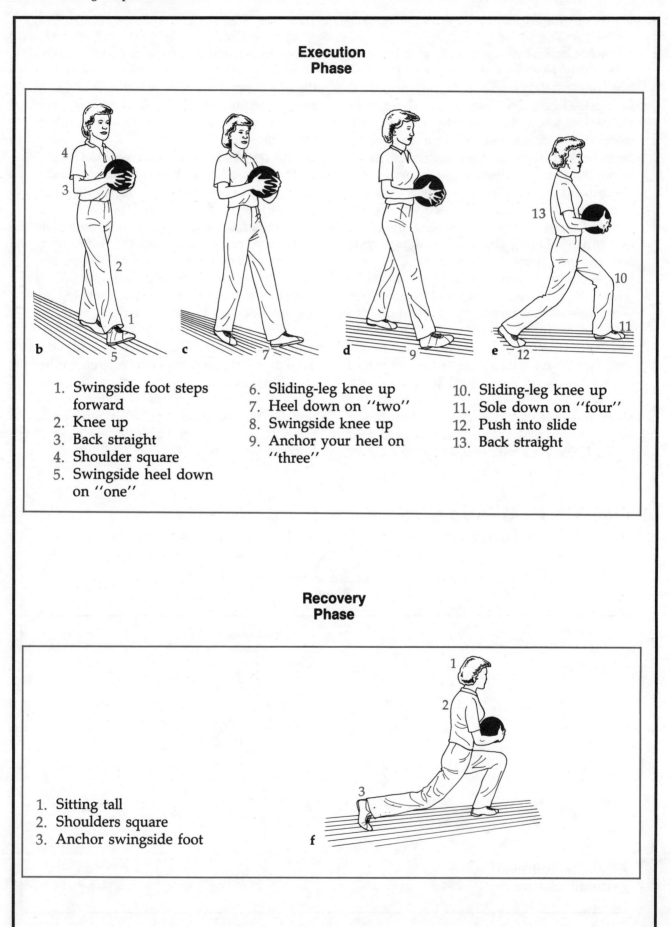

**Execution
Phase**

b

c

d

e

1. Swingside foot steps forward
2. Knee up
3. Back straight
4. Shoulder square
5. Swingside heel down on "one"

6. Sliding-leg knee up
7. Heel down on "two"
8. Swingside knee up
9. Anchor your heel on "three"

10. Sliding-leg knee up
11. Sole down on "four"
12. Push into slide
13. Back straight

**Recovery
Phase**

f

1. Sitting tall
2. Shoulders square
3. Anchor swingside foot

Detecting Footwork, Rhythm, and Gait Errors

Errors in footwork during an actual delivery usually result from (a) an error in timing (rhythm) between the ball and your footwork, (b) an improperly directed pushaway, or (c) an unstable gait. You can eliminate most footwork errors if you learn how to recognize them before they become deeply ingrained. Some common errors and suggestions on how to correct them follow.

ERROR

CORRECTION

1. You take steps too fast.

1. Count through your cadence once before you initiate movement. Fit your steps to the cadence.

2. You take the first step on your toe or with a shuffle.

2. Step out by lifting your foot off the approach just as you would if you were taking a walk. Think to yourself, ''Knee up.''

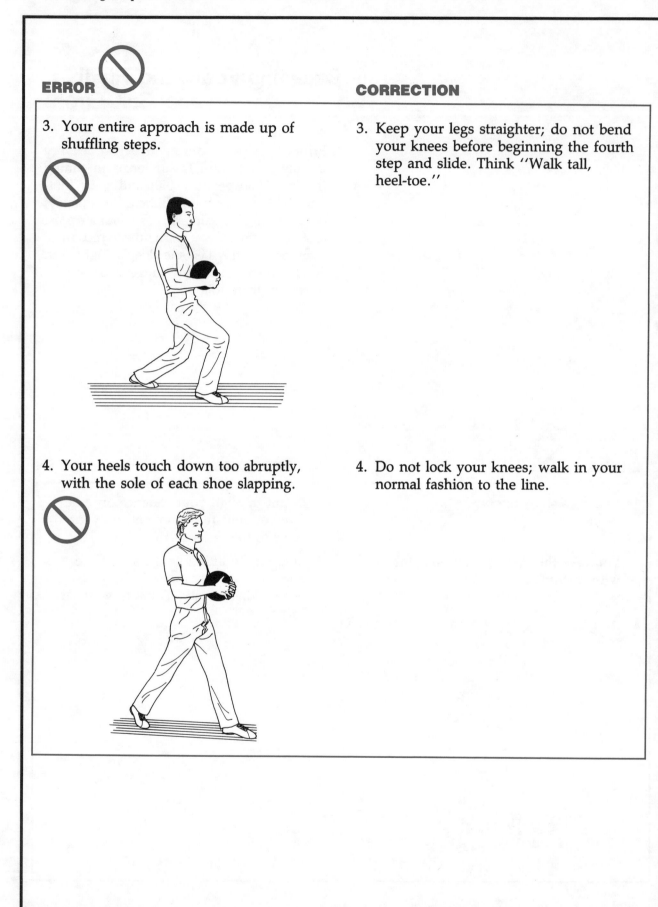

ERROR

CORRECTION

3. Your entire approach is made up of shuffling steps.

3. Keep your legs straighter; do not bend your knees before beginning the fourth step and slide. Think ''Walk tall, heel-toe.''

4. Your heels touch down too abruptly, with the sole of each shoe slapping.

4. Do not lock your knees; walk in your normal fashion to the line.

ERROR   **CORRECTION**

5. You walk too wide a track, too narrow a track, or in a cross-stepping pattern.

5. Allow your feet to trace a path slightly inside each hip and parallel with your swing. Also, check to see that your pushaway is directed in line with your shoulder and the target.

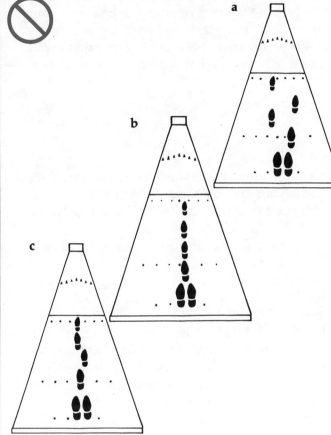

6. You are off balance at the foul line.

6. Keep your back straight, with your swingside knee bending deeply as you push your slide toward the foul line. Think, "Sit tall."

Footwork Drills

These drills all begin from the midline ball setup position. After taking your position on the approach for a normal setup, do not put your fingers in the holes or align the ball with your swing plane. Hold your ball in both hands at your midline, waist-level and touching your body.

Courtesy Tip: You are slowly and systematically performing these drills near others who are bowling. Always check for clearance on either side of you so that you do not annoy others or injure yourself or anyone around you.

1. Power Push

Assume the midline ball setup position standing approximately 4 feet from the foul line. With both feet planted flatly on the approach, and focus your eyes on the second arrow. To sharpen your concept of timing, subdivide your cadence by adding an "AND" count between each number.

On the "AND" after "three," begin lifting your sliding foot off the approach; bend your swingside knee.

On the count of "four," say to yourself, "Push," while touching your sliding sole down in its step forward and bending your swingside leg deeply. Use your swingside sole as an anchor and push your sliding foot forward toward the foul line.

On the "AND" after "four," say to yourself, "Slide." Meanwhile, keep your upper body almost perpendicular to the approach (do not bend forward more than 20 degrees from the vertical); allow your hips to move downward.

Create a mental picture of being on a tightrope, your swingside foot pushing your sliding foot along, both knees bent, your eyes looking down the rope and your chest and shoulders perpendicular to the rope. Hold this "tightrope" position and concentrate on how the muscles of your lower back, buttocks, hips, and thighs feel. Note that your sliding foot has moved into a position under your center of gravity and that you are well balanced. Study the feeling of sitting tall.

Perform this drill 3 times for each characteristic listed in the chart below, then move on to the next characteristic—a total of 12 trials. Give yourself one point for each time you can recall having felt each characteristic.

Characteristic	Trial number		
	1	2	3
Sliding foot push	_____	_____	_____
Back held upright	_____	_____	_____
Swingside knee bend	_____	_____	_____
Good balance	_____	_____	_____

Success Goal = 8 out of 12 possible points

Your Score = (#) _____ total points

2. Full Footwork and Cadence

Take the midline ball setup at your normal setup location at the back of the approach. Begin counting your cadence.

On the "AND" count after "four," step out with your swingside foot.

On "one," touch the swingside heel down on the approach. Take normal heel–toe walking steps and concentrate on the feeling of your weight being transferred from the heel, through the arch, and to the toe as you walk forward. *Note*: Do not place one foot in front of the other as in walking a straight line, do not step side-to-side, and do not cross one foot in front of the other.

On the count of "two," touch your sliding foot heel down on the approach.

On "three," keep your knees straight and anchor your swingside heel on the approach in preparation for the power push to the finish position. Notice the feeling of walking tall.

On "four," push your sliding foot forward, using your swingside foot as the anchor on the approach. Incorporate the power push and focus your attention on the feel of the push and its effect on your hips and bowling shoulder.

Note: Although each step falls precisely on a count of your cadence, your motions should flow together. Do not hesitate between steps. The time between steps is the same; the third and fourth steps are taken no faster than the first and second.

Perform this drill 3 times for each characteristic listed in the chart below then move on to the next characteristic—a total of 15 trials. Give yourself one point for each time you can recall having felt each characteristic.

Characteristic	Trial number		
	1	2	3
Timing of steps	_____	_____	_____
Sliding foot push	_____	_____	_____
Back held upright	_____	_____	_____
Swingside knee bend	_____	_____	_____
Good balance	_____	_____	_____

Success Goal = 10 out of 15 possible points

Your Score = (#) _____ total points

3. Starting Position Check

After achieving some footwork consistency in the previous drills, you are now ready to make a precise determination of how far from the foul line you should start your well-executed approach. The conventional method is to pace off four normal walking steps and add a half-step for the slide; this has been assumed to be the appropriate length for the approach. However, this method is undesirable because it does not allow enough room for a sufficiently long push and slide.

Perform the previous footwork drill again, noting how far your sliding toe stops from the foul line each time. Mark this location off to one side with a ruler, piece of paper, or other small object. Be careful not to step on it and slip.

After several repetitions, checking the quality of your footwork and push and repositioning the marker each time, measure the distance of the marker from the foul line. Walk back to your original starting position and establish your new starting position this distance closer to the foul line. From this new position, make five more footwork trials ending with the push; see how close your sliding toe is to the foul line. If necessary, adjust your starting position to allow your sliding toe to stop 2 to 4 inches from the line. Remember this new position well; write it down if necessary. This will be your new starting position for the remainder of this text.

Repeat the previous drill 10 times, using your personalized starting position. Give yourself credit for each well-executed footwork drill in which you stop 2 to 4 inches from the foul line.

Success Goal = 8 out of 10 well-executed, well-spaced footwork patterns

Your Score = (#) _____ well-executed patterns

Proper Footwork
Keys to Success Checklist

Before you attempt to add any upper-body movements to the footwork, you must be sure that you are taking heel–toe steps that are so closely timed with your pendulum swing cadence that you gain a strong, well-balanced finish position. To help you sharpen these skills, ask your teacher, coach, or a trained observer to qualitatively evaluate your technique according to the checklist that follows.

Preparation
Phase

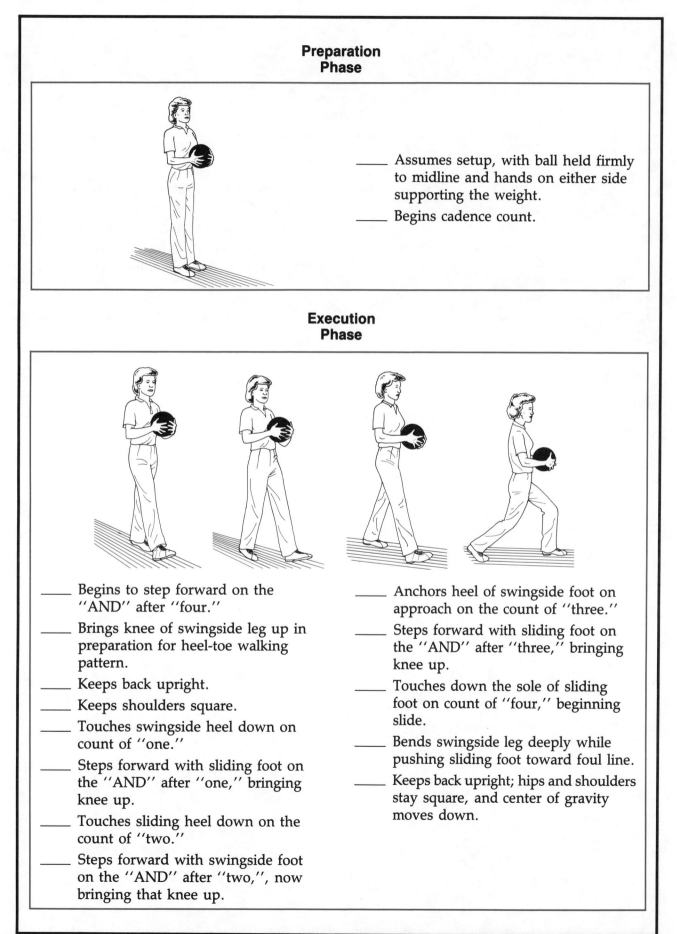

_____ Assumes setup, with ball held firmly to midline and hands on either side supporting the weight.

_____ Begins cadence count.

Execution
Phase

_____ Begins to step forward on the "AND" after "four."

_____ Brings knee of swingside leg up in preparation for heel-toe walking pattern.

_____ Keeps back upright.

_____ Keeps shoulders square.

_____ Touches swingside heel down on count of "one."

_____ Steps forward with sliding foot on the "AND" after "one," bringing knee up.

_____ Touches sliding heel down on the count of "two."

_____ Steps forward with swingside foot on the "AND" after "two,", now bringing that knee up.

_____ Anchors heel of swingside foot on approach on the count of "three."

_____ Steps forward with sliding foot on the "AND" after "three," bringing knee up.

_____ Touches down the sole of sliding foot on count of "four," beginning slide.

_____ Bends swingside leg deeply while pushing sliding foot toward foul line.

_____ Keeps back upright; hips and shoulders stay square, and center of gravity moves down.

Recovery
Phase

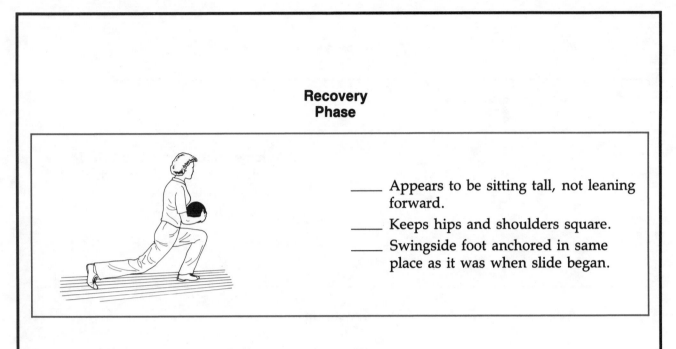

_____ Appears to be sitting tall, not leaning forward.

_____ Keeps hips and shoulders square.

_____ Swingside foot anchored in same place as it was when slide began.

Step 4 Utility Delivery

A utility delivery allows you to connect your footwork to the pendulum swing in delivering the ball. At this point, details of the mechanics of the delivery are purposefully omitted so that you can get an overview of a four-step delivery.

WHY IS THE UTILITY DELIVERY IMPORTANT?

To help you learn faster, you should be bowling complete games as soon as possible. You can use your utility delivery as a framework upon which to build the techniques you will learn in later steps.

HOW TO EXECUTE A UTILITY DELIVERY

Assume a normal setup at the appropriate location at the back of the approach. Begin counting your cadence.

Midway between a count of four and the next count of one, begin pushing your ball straight forward and stepping forward with your swingside foot so that your elbows lock and your swingside heel makes contact on the

count of "one." Let your ball fall into the downswing from this extended arm position and keep walking; do not hesitate. Allow your movements to flow together into one graceful sequence while continuing to count to yourself.

Take your first three steps in a heel-toe walking fashion, making your heels touch down on the approach precisely on a count. Keep your upper body upright to avoid taking your steps on your toes; do not bend over at the waist.

As you begin your fourth step, deeply bend your swingside knee as you touch down the toe of your sliding foot on the approach. Push the sliding foot forward, using the swingside foot as an anchor. Allow your hips to lower as you keep your back upright.

Let your ball roll off of your hand during your slide and allow your bowling arm to complete the arc of the swing; this motion is the follow-through. Try to stay in this position, with your bowling arm held high, until the ball is halfway down the lane. Figure 4.1 shows how to execute a utility delivery.

Figure 4.1 Keys to Success: Utility Delivery

Preparation Phase

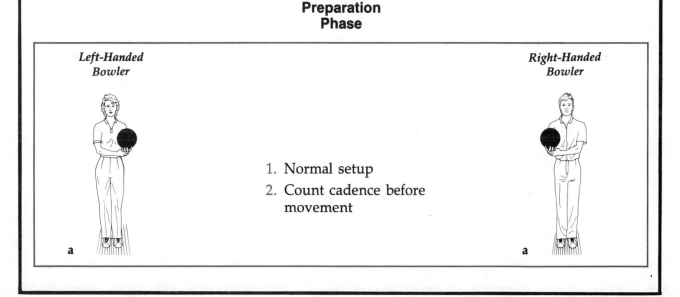

Left-Handed Bowler

Right-Handed Bowler

1. Normal setup
2. Count cadence before movement

a

a

Execution
Phase

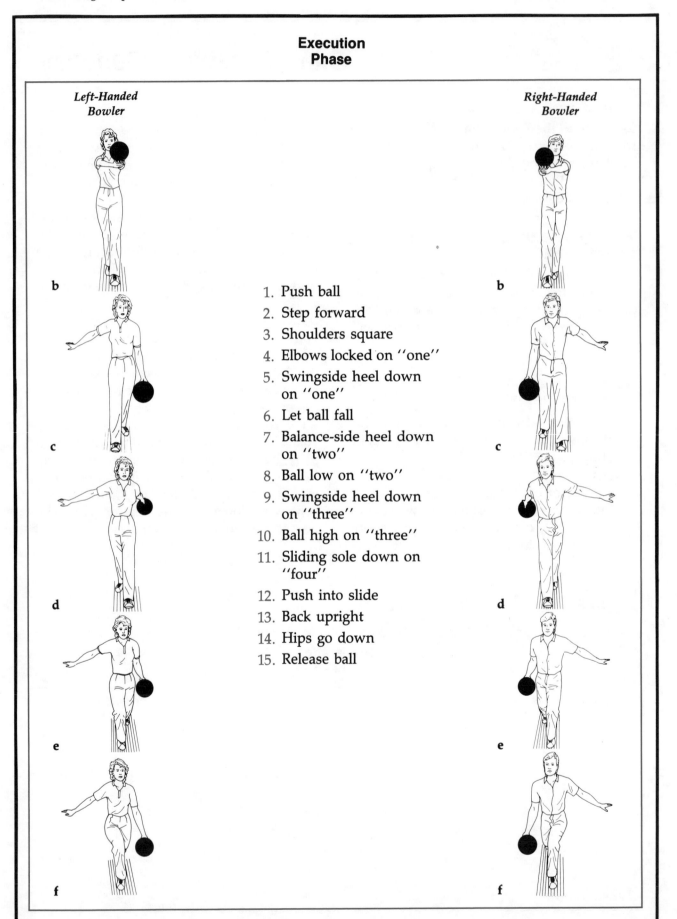

Left-Handed Bowler

Right-Handed Bowler

1. Push ball
2. Step forward
3. Shoulders square
4. Elbows locked on "one"
5. Swingside heel down on "one"
6. Let ball fall
7. Balance-side heel down on "two"
8. Ball low on "two"
9. Swingside heel down on "three"
10. Ball high on "three"
11. Sliding sole down on "four"
12. Push into slide
13. Back upright
14. Hips go down
15. Release ball

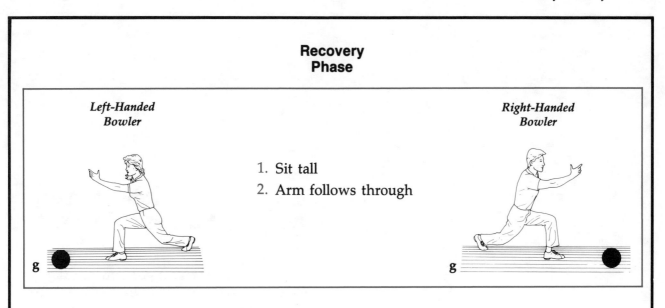

**Recovery
Phase**

*Left-Handed
Bowler*

*Right-Handed
Bowler*

1. Sit tall
2. Arm follows through

Utility Delivery Drill

Utility Delivery

Assume your normal setup at your appropriate location at the back of the approach. Begin counting your cadence. Follow the Utility Delivery Keys to Success in Figure 4.1. Adjust the speed of your count until it is close to your normal walking pace. Do not hesitate between steps. Take all steps at the same pace. Do not worry if you feel awkward. With successive attempts, your movements will become more comfortable.

Begin to push your ball with both hands directly in line with your bowling shoulder and start stepping forward with your swingside foot at the same time.

When both arms are straight out and your swingside heel has touched down, let your ball fall (swing) down freely and keep walking, taking two more steps and a slide. The proper positions are:

Step #	Ball position	Foot in front
1	Straight out in front	Swingside (heel down)
2	Straight down	Balance side (heel down)
3	Straight out in back	Swingside (heel down)
4 (slide)	Straight down	Balance side (toe down)

After rolling the minimum number of balls for this drill, feel free to increase the Success Goal, as necessary, to feel comfortable with your utility delivery.

Success Goal = 20 utility deliveries

Your Score = (#) _____ deliveries

Utility Delivery
Keys to Success Checklist

To make sure that you perform the utility delivery correctly, ask your teacher, coach, or a trained observer to briefly check your technique according to the checklist below. Eliminate poor habits now before you attempt to add any other techniques.

Preparation Phase

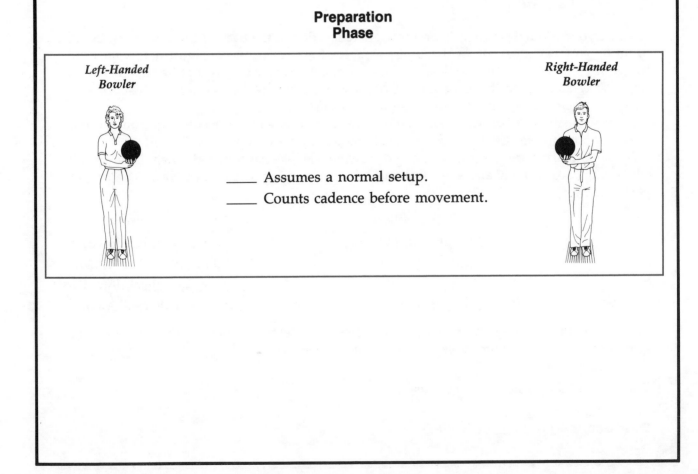

Left-Handed Bowler

Right-Handed Bowler

_____ Assumes a normal setup.
_____ Counts cadence before movement.

Execution
Phase

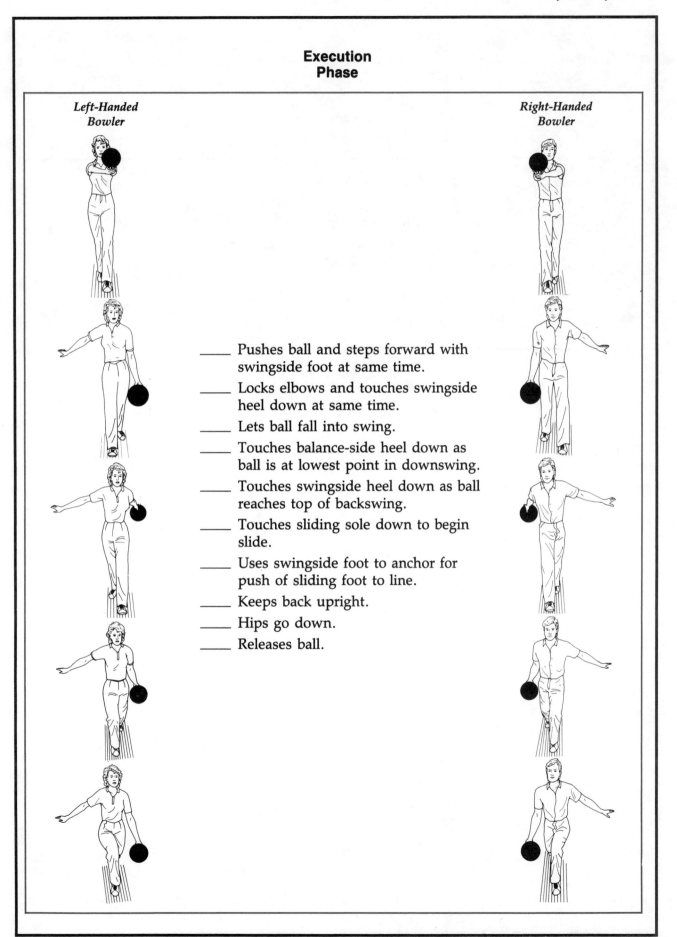

Left-Handed Bowler

Right-Handed Bowler

_____ Pushes ball and steps forward with swingside foot at same time.

_____ Locks elbows and touches swingside heel down at same time.

_____ Lets ball fall into swing.

_____ Touches balance-side heel down as ball is at lowest point in downswing.

_____ Touches swingside heel down as ball reaches top of backswing.

_____ Touches sliding sole down to begin slide.

_____ Uses swingside foot to anchor for push of sliding foot to line.

_____ Keeps back upright.

_____ Hips go down.

_____ Releases ball.

Recovery
Phase

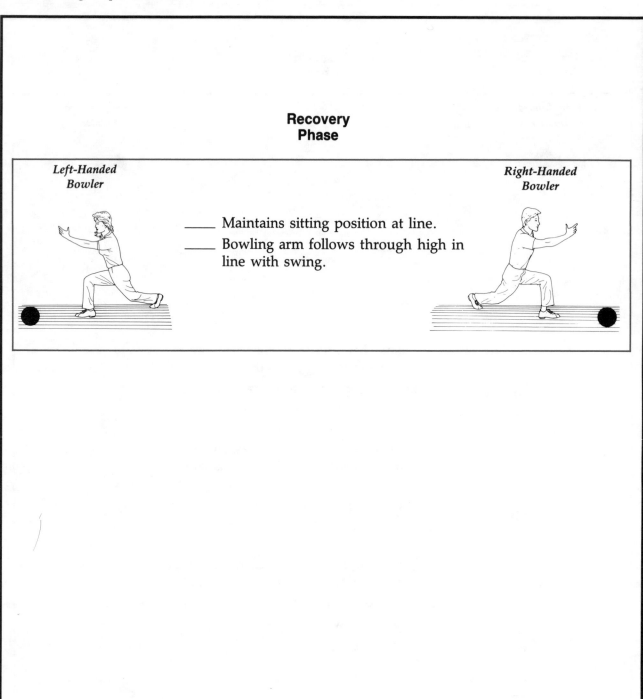

Left-Handed Bowler

_____ Maintains sitting position at line.
_____ Bowling arm follows through high in line with swing.

Right-Handed Bowler

Step 5   Ball Dynamics

Ball *dynamics* are the collective skidding and rolling motions of a bowling ball as it proceeds down the lane toward the pins. The way a ball visibly acts on the lane is popularly called a *ball reaction*. Under the category of dynamics are the two reaction types called the *straight ball* and the *hook ball*. You will learn the techniques of delivering both.

The straight ball travels a straight path from your hand to the desired, or *object*, pin. The straight ball will be introduced first because it is the best model for learning the high-leverage release without having the hand and arm positioning problems commonly encountered by inexperienced bowlers attempting to roll the hook.

The hook ball travels a bent, outside-to-inside path from your hand to the object pin. You will learn the hook ball after the straight ball so that you can systematically build your hook ball skills on those developed with the straight ball (see Figure 5.1a,b).

Two poor alternatives to the hook ball are often described in bowling texts; you will not practice throwing these, but they are mentioned so that you can identify them. One is the *backup ball*, or *reverse hook*, and the other is *curve ball* (see Figure 5.1c,d).

The backup ball veers from the bowler's inside to his or her outside. It is rolled with the fingers held pointed at approximately the 3 o'clock (9 o'clock for a left-handed bowler) position at the release (see Figure 5.2).

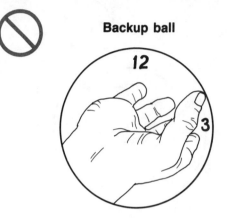

Backup ball

Figure 5.2 Clockface diagram of hand position used to deliver a backup ball.

Note that the clockface terminology used in describing hand positions always refers to the direction in which the tips of the bowling fingers are pointing, not the thumb. It is also from the bowler's perspective.

The curve ball no longer exists in practice. It was rolled by the bowler turning the wrist from the outside to the inside at the instant of release (see Figue 5.3a,b). Although possible on oiled shellac- or lacquer-covered lane surfaces,

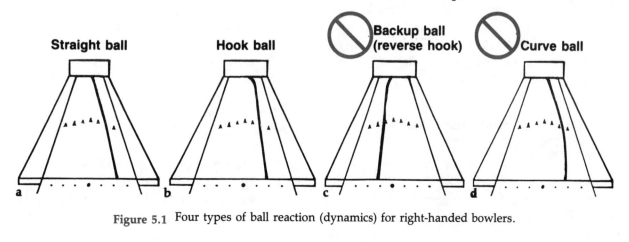

Figure 5.1 Four types of ball reaction (dynamics) for right-handed bowlers.

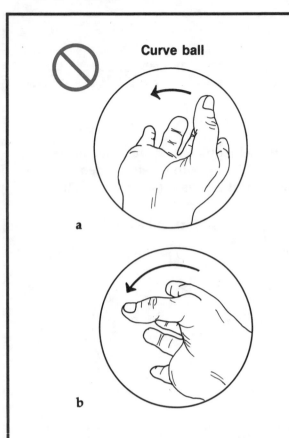

Curve ball

a

b

Figure 5.3 Clockface diagrams of hand positions used to deliver a curve ball.

its dynamics are not possible on present-day, oiled urethane lane surfaces.

But regardless of how the lane surface is finished, a ball that is used often by the same bowler will begin to show a ball track. A *ball track* is a ring of scratches that develops on the surface of the ball with use; these scratches mark the area of most frequent contact with the lane. It is possible to roll a straight ball or a hook ball with any type of ball track. The diameter of the ball track varies from one bowler to another, ranging from very small (a *spinner*) to intermediate (a *semiroller*) to the full circumference of the ball (a *full roller*) (see Figure 5.4).

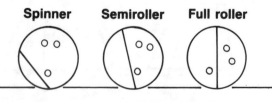

Spinner   **Semiroller**   **Full roller**

Figure 5.4 Range of ball tracks (right-handed bowler).

WHY ARE STRAIGHT AND HOOK BALLS BOTH IMPORTANT?

A straight ball, besides its worth to the beginner, is often a valuable alternative for any bowler who finds that the hook ball is unreliable on a *difficult lane condition*, an unusual state of friction between the ball and the lane surface. In such a case, the bowler may be unsuccessful in using a hook ball to strike or spare; the straight ball may be significantly easier to control.

However, a hook ball is the best strike ball because it knocks down, or *carries*, 10 pins more effectively. Therefore, it is preferred by professional bowlers. Although the hook ball is more sensitive to variations in lane conditions than the straight ball, the greater striking power of the hook ball compensates for such a disadvantage, particularly on less difficult lane conditions.

The major reason that the hook ball carries pins better is that it involves a steeper *angle of attack* into the *pocket* (the desired point of impact for a strike). The angle of attack is formed by two imaginary lines: one drawn straight down the 17th board (1-3 pocket for right-handed bowlers; 1-2 pocket for left-handed bowlers) and the other drawn in line with the direction in which the ball is rolling (see Figure 5.5). In the case of a straight ball, the angle of attack can be no greater than that formed by a line drawn down the 17th board and one from the outer edge of the lane at the foul line to the strike pocket. The hook affords a steeper angle because the ball is rolling into the pocket from a point closer to the pins—the *break point*, the point at which the ball begins to hook.

The steeper angle of attack lessens the effect of *deflection*—the deviation of the ball path after an off-center impact with a pin—by increasing the chance of the ball to hit the 5 pin, or *kingpin*, which sits directly behind the 1 pin, or *headpin* (see Figure 5.6).

Another reason the hook ball has greater carrying power is that it makes pins tilt and spin more upon impact than does a straight ball. Although a straight ball rolling through a rack of pins imparts some rotation to the pins which it contacts, much more pin action

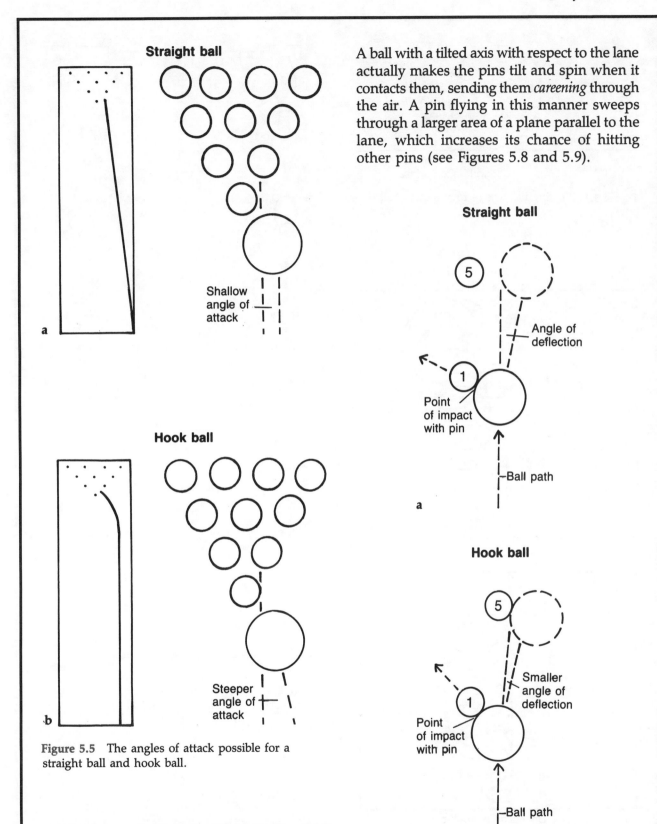

A ball with a tilted axis with respect to the lane actually makes the pins tilt and spin when it contacts them, sending them *careening* through the air. A pin flying in this manner sweeps through a larger area of a plane parallel to the lane, which increases its chance of hitting other pins (see Figures 5.8 and 5.9).

Figure 5.5 The angles of attack possible for a straight ball and hook ball.

Figure 5.6 The angles of deflection resulting from a straight ball and a hook ball.

results from a hook ball with a tilted *axis of rotation*. The axis of rotation, popularly called simply the *axis*, is a line passing through the center of the ball and through the center of a plane formed by the ball track (see Figure 5.7).

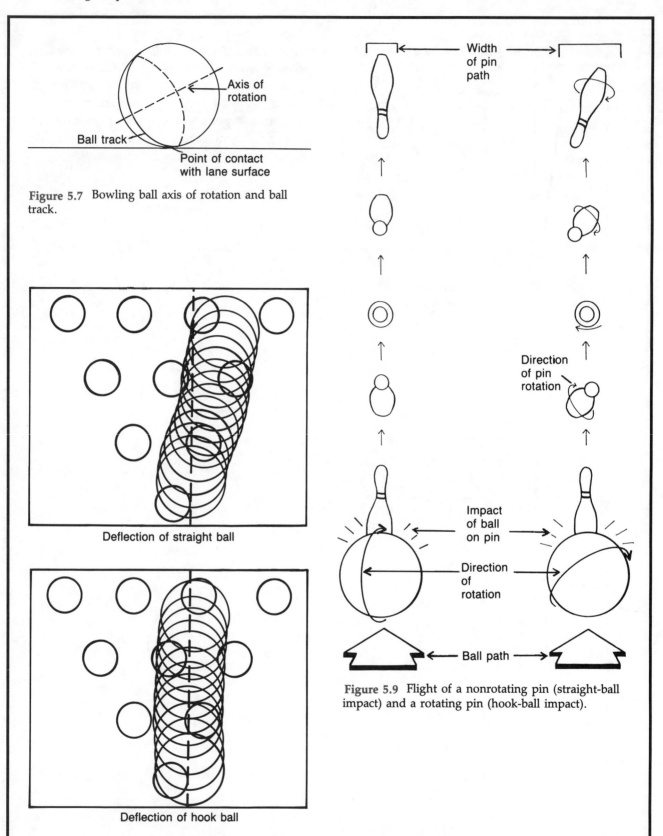

Figure 5.7 Bowling ball axis of rotation and ball track.

Deflection of straight ball

Deflection of hook ball

Figure 5.8 Deflection path of straight and hook balls rolling through a rack of pins.

Width of pin path

Direction of pin rotation

Impact of ball on pin

Direction of rotation

Ball path

Figure 5.9 Flight of a nonrotating pin (straight-ball impact) and a rotating pin (hook-ball impact).

CHOOSING BETWEEN STRAIGHT AND HOOK BALLS

Once mastered, the hook ball should be used for strikes whenever possible. The straight ball is usually more reliable for most spares, although a completely uniform lane condition, one with equal friction over the entire lane surface, allows equal spare efficiency with the hook ball. However, a completely uniform lane condition is rare.

A wooden lane is usually covered with a urethane coating (*lane finish*), which is protected from ball abrasion by a daily application of oil (*lane dressing*) (see Figure 5.10). Ball reaction is remarkably dependent on the amount and location of the dressing on the lane and the state of repair of the lane finish.

If a lane condition is *hooking* (*slow, high-friction*); *slick* (*fast, low-friction*); or *spotty* (a mixture of high- and low-friction areas), a hook ball may act unpredictably, with strikes occurring less frequently and splits and multiple-pin spare leaves (pins left standing) increasing in frequency. In such a case, switching to a straight ball—playing it safe—would allow better control and consistency. In sum, the hook ball is preferred on well-maintained lane conditions, whereas the straight ball is more reliable on difficult lane conditions.

There are two major reasons why a straight ball may be more reliable on difficult lane conditions. First, in a properly rolled straight ball, lift is applied by the fingers in line with the desired ball path; this action tends to dynam-

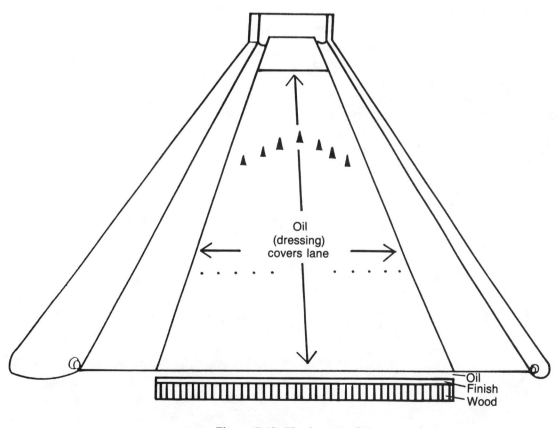

Figure 5.10 The lane condition.

ically stabilize the ball in the direction it is rolling. Second, because the straight-ball delivery requires the hand to stay behind the ball—therefore, closer to the body—more of the body's momentum can be transferred to the ball at the release. This gives the ball more forward speed and makes it more resistant to deviation by lane-surface irregularities. However, to maximize pin carry, a straight ball must begin to roll soon after touchdown on the lane surface; it should not be skidding, a dynamic that makes the ball easier to deflect upon impact with a pin.

For more information on lane conditions and adjustments to them, see Allen and Ritger (1981), Strickland (1980), and Weber and Alexander (1981).

HOW TO EXECUTE THE STRAIGHT-BALL DELIVERY

To execute the straight-ball delivery, take a normal setup at your usual location on the approach, using the assigned visual target. Swing and roll the ball with your palm up and your gripping fingers pointed toward 12 o'clock (see Figure 5.11). Keep your elbow *hinge*, the direction in which your elbow bends, perpendicular to your swing (see Figure 5.12). Keep your wrist firm in the 180-degree, extended position. Use your *supporting fingers*, your index and little fingers, to help. This action will make your thumb *clear* (leave its hole) more

Figure 5.12 Elbow hinge with fingers in straight-ball position.

easily. After your thumb has cleared and just before the lifting motion, curl your fingers.

Make a mental picture of squeezing a rubber ball with only your fingers during your release and follow-through. Note that your thumb is straight—not curled (see Figure 5.13). The squeeze will assist you in lifting your ball up and out and onto the lane surface so that it will roll directly in line with the desired ball path.

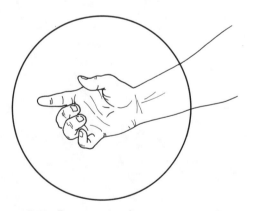

Figure 5.13 Proper grip; fingers squeeze, but thumb does not.

Keep your fingertips in the 12-o'clock position until you complete your follow-through. Your elbow hinge should remain perpendicular to your swing. Maintain the firm wrist (see Figure 5.14).

In your final recovery position, your fingers should still be at 12 o'clock in the follow-through, with the back of your bowling hand

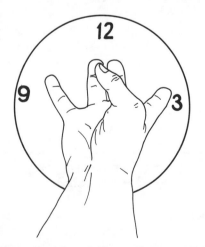

Figure 5.11 Clockface diagram of the straight-ball hand position.

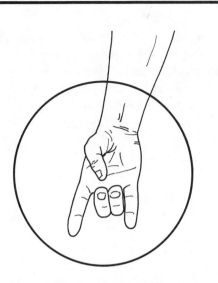

Figure 5.14 The straight-ball release.

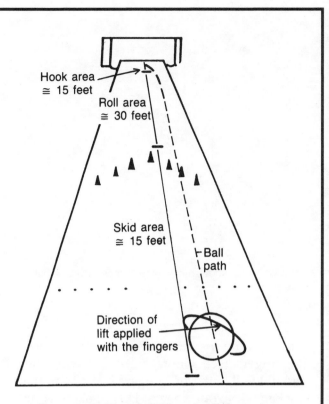

Figure 5.15 Hook-ball lift and roll dynamics.

high and presenting itself to the pins. Your fingers should be curled. Your eyes should still be bonded to your target. Though normally this pose is held until the ball is halfway to the pins, this time, hold your well-balanced position until the ball makes contact with the pins, and observe the ball dynamics.

HOW TO EXECUTE
THE HOOK-BALL DELIVERY

You accomplish the hook by imparting lift in a direction *not* in line with the ball path, so that the ball will skid farther down the lane. It will begin its roll into the pins from the break point (see Figure 5.15).

To execute the hook-ball delivery, take a setup at your usual location on the approach, using the assigned visual target. Swing and roll the ball with your palm up and your gripping fingers pointed about 45 degrees to the inside of your swing plane. This will mean a finger position of 10 o'clock for a right-handed bowler, 2 o'clock for a left-handed bowler (see Figure 5.16). Hold your hand firmly in this position as you swing and deliver your ball. It is absolutely essential that you keep your elbow hinge perpendicular to your swing throughout your delivery and follow-through (see Figure 5.17).

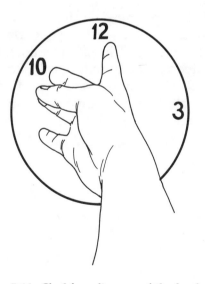

Figure 5.16 Clockface diagram of the hook-ball hand position.

Figure 5.17 Elbow hinge with fingers in hook-ball position.

Keep your wrist firm and use your supporting fingers (see Figure 5.18). As with the straight ball, curl your fingers just as you lift the ball with your fingers. Do not allow your hand, your forearm, or your upper arm to rotate. Although the hook ball possesses some *spin*, horizontal rotation, this spin should be produced only by your lifting fingers held stably in the prescribed position—not by your hand turning at the wrist or your arm at the shoulder or elbow. The effective hook ball is still a predominantly rolling ball. Roll your hook ball at exactly the same speed as your straight ball; do not, by any means, speed up or slow down your ball to obtain a hook.

In your final recovery position, your fingers should still be at a 45-degree angle to the inside position. Your fingers should be curled; use the squeeze described previously. Your eyes should still be bonded to your target. Hold this well-balanced position until the ball

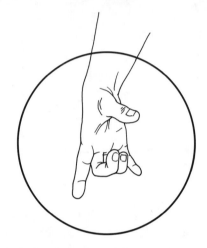

Figure 5.18 The hook-ball release.

makes contact with the pins. Your elbow hinge should remain perpendicular to your swing, and your wrist should be firm. Figure 5.19 shows the Keys to Success for effective straight and hook ball dynamics.

Figure 5.19 Keys to Success:
Ball Dynamics

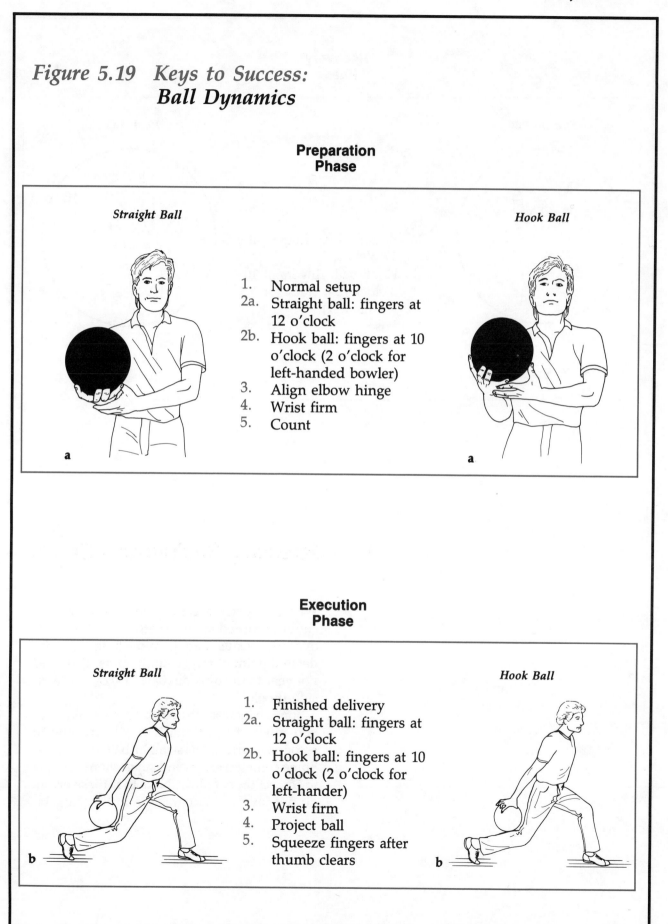

**Preparation
Phase**

Straight Ball   *Hook Ball*

1. Normal setup
2a. Straight ball: fingers at 12 o'clock
2b. Hook ball: fingers at 10 o'clock (2 o'clock for left-handed bowler)
3. Align elbow hinge
4. Wrist firm
5. Count

a   a

**Execution
Phase**

Straight Ball   *Hook Ball*

1. Finished delivery
2a. Straight ball: fingers at 12 o'clock
2b. Hook ball: fingers at 10 o'clock (2 o'clock for left-hander)
3. Wrist firm
4. Project ball
5. Squeeze fingers after thumb clears

b   b

**Recovery
Phase**

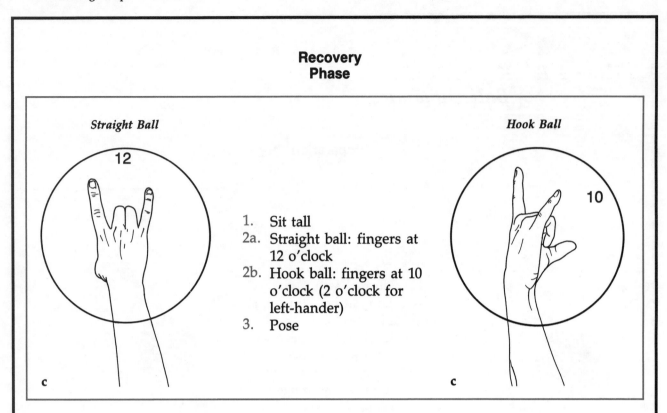

Straight Ball

12

Hook Ball

10

1. Sit tall
2a. Straight ball: fingers at 12 o'clock
2b. Hook ball: fingers at 10 o'clock (2 o'clock for left-hander)
3. Pose

c

c

Detecting Straight-Ball Errors

When properly executed, your straight ball should proceed along a path from the hand, over the visual target, and straight to the desired point of impact at the pins. It should not veer to the outside (back up) or to the inside (hook).

You can increase the consistency with which you roll a straight ball if you learn how to recognize errors in straight-ball dynamics. Some common errors and suggestions on how to correct them follow. Note that these errors do not involve inaccuracy in hitting targets.

ERROR 🚫

1. Ball veers off to one side of the lane instead of going straight along the desired path.

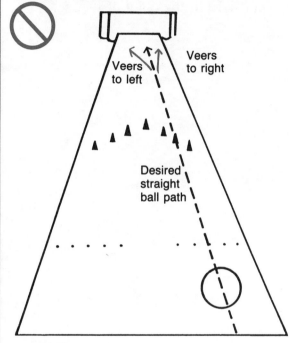

CORRECTION

1. Make sure that your fingers are held at 12 o'clock, your wrist is firm, and your elbow hinge is locked in line with your swing plane.

2. Ball seems to be skidding or sliding instead of rolling.

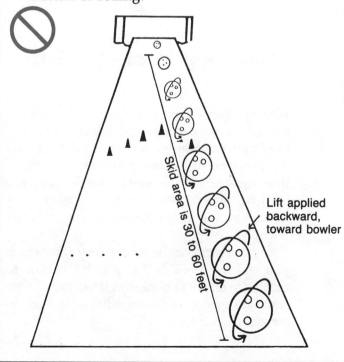

2. Keep your wrist firm and push into your finish. Feel your shoulder push, your elbow lock, your thumb clear, and your fingers lift the ball up and onto the lane surface. Your thumb may be *hanging* in the thumbhole, so have a trained person check your ball fit.

ERROR   **CORRECTION**

3. If you hear a "thump, thump," the ball is rolling over the grip holes.

3. Check and correct your finger position, your wrist firmness, and the ball fit. Keep your elbow locked. Do not rotate your wrist at the point of release.

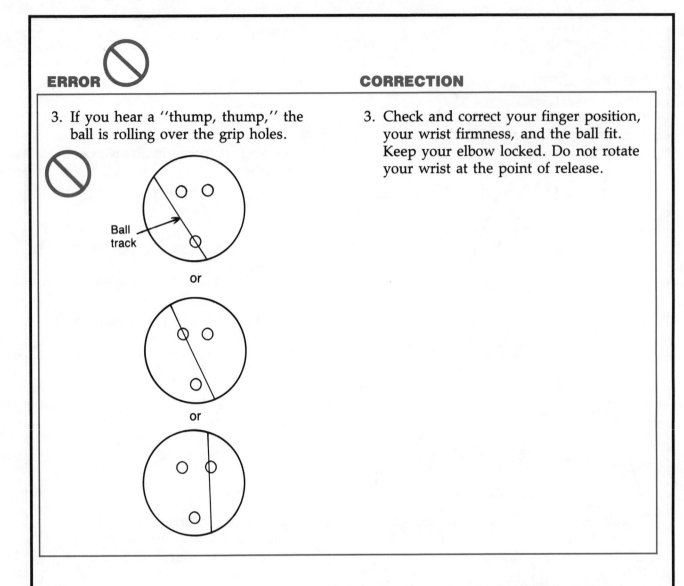

Detecting Hook-Ball Errors

When properly executed, the hook ball should proceed along a straight path from the hand, over the visual target, and down the lane. At the break point, approximately two-thirds to three-quarters of the way down the lane, the hook ball should veer toward the inside of the lane on its way to the desired point of impact with the object pins.

You can increase the consistency with which you roll the hook ball if you learn how to recognize errors in hook-ball dynamics. Some common errors and suggestions on how to correct them follow.

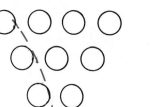

ERROR

CORRECTION

1. Ball misses either the target point, the desired point of impact with the pins, or both.

1. Make sure that your fingers are not held too far toward the inside (8 or 9 o'clock for a right-handed bowler, 3 or 4 o'clock for a left-hander). This would allow your arm to move too far away from the body, making the ball touch down too far to the outside. Have a trained observer check your delivery.

Miss to the inside

Miss to the outside

Desired strike ball path

Four ways of missing the target point

Desired target point

Desired ball path

Miss to the inside

Miss to the outside

ERROR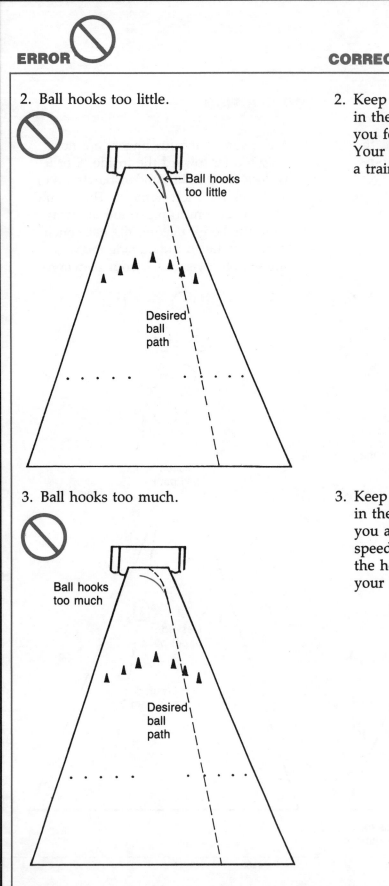

CORRECTION

2. Ball hooks too little.

2. Keep your wrist firm and your fingers in the proper position. Make sure that you feel good leverage at the release. Your thumb may be hanging, so have a trained person check your ball fit.

3. Ball hooks too much.

3. Keep your wrist firm and your fingers in the proper position. Make sure that you are rolling the ball at normal speed. Your fingers may be hanging in the holes; have a trained person check your ball fit.

4. Ball hooks inconsistently.

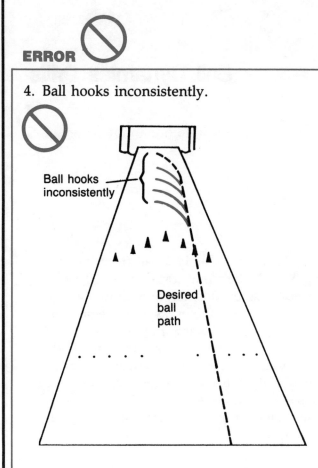

Ball hooks
inconsistently

Desired
ball
path

4. Keep your wrist firm and your fingers in the proper position. Be sure that you are rolling your ball at the same speed every time.

5. Ball rolls over the grip holes (see Straight-Ball Error 3).

5. Check and correct your finger position, your wrist firmness, and the ball fit. Keep your elbow locked. Do not rotate your wrist to the inside or the outside at the release.

Ball Dynamics Drills

Courtesy Tip: Always check for clearance on either side so that you do not annoy others or injure yourself or anyone around you.

1. *High-Leverage Straight-Ball Finish*

Assume a normal setup with your ball, but stand only approximately 4 feet from the foul line. Begin your cadence, focus on your visual target, and take a one-step delivery. To execute a one-step delivery, push the ball straight from the setup position and allow the ball to fall into the pendulum swing; when the ball reaches the top of the backswing, begin your power push (see Step 3, Drill 1), and allow the ball to swing forward; then release it.

During your finish, focus your attention on the *leverage linkage* among the following body segments. Just like a chain, your sliding foot is linked to its knee and hip. Your hip is linked through your stably held back to your bowling shoulder. If your timing is good, the leverage linkage among all of the involved body segments is solid at the instant you lift and project your ball onto the lane. You should feel more pressure on your lifting fingers (you have your "fingers in the shot"). You should also feel your bowling shoulder support your straight bowling arm (you have your "shoulder in your shot").

Because the straight-ball hand position places your lifting fingers closer to your sliding foot, you can use this drill to learn the feel of increasingly greater leverage as you attain better timing between your swing and your slide. Do not be concerned with where your ball hits the pins.

Perform three well-executed one-step deliveries for each of the characteristics in the following chart, giving yourself one point each time you felt a characteristic.

Success Goal = 18 one-step straight-ball deliveries

Characteristic	Trial number		
	1	2	3
Foot, knee, and hip solid	_____	_____	_____
Back held stable	_____	_____	_____
Firm wrist at release	_____	_____	_____
Push with shoulder	_____	_____	_____
Squeeze with fingers	_____	_____	_____
Fingers at 12 o'clock	_____	_____	_____

Your Score = (#) _____ one-step straight-ball deliveries

2. Full Straight-Ball Delivery

Assume your normal setup position and take a flowing, well-executed delivery, rolling a straight ball over your visual target. End with a high-leverage lift, a finish, and a follow-through as explained in the utility delivery. Every time you return from the foul line, ask yourself whether you felt that your fingers and your shoulder were in your shot. If you did not, you lost leverage at some stage in your delivery.

The most probable errors are late pushaway, early pushaway, not keeping your back straight and your body in a sitting-tall posture, a tentative, or *fluffy*, balance arm (allowing a dropped bowling shoulder), and a nonsupportive, or *broken*, wrist. If you think you are making one or more of these errors, don't worry because you'll learn to identify and correct these errors as you refine your technique.

Perform three well-executed deliveries for each of the characteristics in the following chart, giving yourself one point each time you felt a characteristic. Try to correct any errors you detect.

Success Goal = 24 straight-ball deliveries

Characteristic	Trial number		
	1	2	3
Foot, knee, and hip solid	____	____	____
Back held stable	____	____	____
Ball and foot in time	____	____	____
Firm wrist at release	____	____	____
Push with shoulder	____	____	____
Stable balance arm	____	____	____
Squeeze with fingers	____	____	____
Fingers at 12 o'clock	____	____	____

Your Score = (#) ____ straight-ball deliveries

3. Hook-Ball Finish

The objectives of this drill are to show you the hook-ball hand position and to help you build consistency into your hook-ball release.

Assume a normal setup, but stand only approximately 4 feet from the foul line. Align your bowling elbow hinge perpendicular to your intended swing plane, then move your fingers 45 degrees to the inside of the 12 o'clock position; keep your wrist firm and straight. It is absolutely vital to your consistency that your elbow hinge remains perfectly perpendicular to your swing, even though your fingers are not!

Begin your cadence, focus on your visual target, and take a one-step delivery, using the hook-ball hand position (Figures 5.15 through 5.19).

During your finish, focus your attention on the leverage linkage among your body segments as described in Drill 1. If your swing and slide are in time with one another, you should feel that your lifting fingers and your bowling shoulder are in the shot during your hook-ball release.

Perform five well-executed one-step deliveries for each of the characteristics in the following chart, giving yourself one point each time you felt a characteristic.

Right-Handed

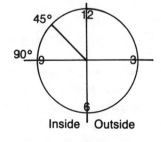

Left-Handed

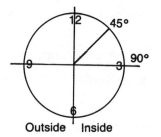

Success Goal = 18 one-step hook-ball deliveries

Characteristic	Trial number		
	1	2	3
Foot, knee, and hip solid	_____	_____	_____
Back held stable	_____	_____	_____
Firm wrist at release	_____	_____	_____
Push with shoulder	_____	_____	_____
Squeeze with fingers	_____	_____	_____
Fingers 45 degrees inside	_____	_____	_____

Your Score = (#) _____ one-step hook-ball deliveries

4. Full Hook-Ball Delivery

Assume your normal setup and take a flowing, well-executed delivery, rolling your hook ball over your visual target. End with a high-leverage lift finish and follow-through as developed in the previous drill.

Every time you return from the foul line, ask yourself whether you felt that your fingers and shoulder were in your shot. If you did not, you lost leverage at some stage in your delivery.

Likely errors are late pushaway, early pushaway, not keeping your back straight and your body in a sitting-tall posture, and a fluffy balance arm (allowing a dropped bowling shoulder). In addition, you might have moved your fingers to a more inside position, a motion called "coming around the ball." Perhaps you broke your wrist back, yielding to the additional force instead of increasing wrist firmness by pushing with your supporting fingers. These errors are subconscious reactions that you must overcome consciously when you later refine your technique.

Perform 3 well-executed deliveries for each of the characteristics in the following chart, giving yourself 1 point each time you felt a characteristic. Try to correct any errors you detect.

Success Goal = 24 hook-ball deliveries

Characteristic	Trial number		
	1	2	3
Foot, knee, and hip solid	_____	_____	_____
Back held stable	_____	_____	_____
Ball and foot in time	_____	_____	_____
Firm wrist at release	_____	_____	_____
Push with shoulder	_____	_____	_____
Stable balance arm	_____	_____	_____
Squeeze with fingers	_____	_____	_____
Fingers 45 degrees inside	_____	_____	_____

Your Score = (#) _____ hook-ball deliveries

5. Marked Axis Dynamics Awareness

You can actually see the difference between straight and hook balls by watching your ball's axis of rotation.

Examine your ball and find your ball track. Lightly mark this track with a white or yellow wax pencil. Next, find and mark the "center" of the circle formed by the track; this center is the *negative axis pole*, the axis pole that will be directed away from the headpin as the ball is rolling down the lane. Directly through the center of the ball, on the opposite side, you will find the *positive axis pole*, the axis pole directed toward the headpin as the ball rolls down the lane. The imaginary line connecting the two poles and running through the center of the ball is the axis of rotation.

Mark the positive axis pole. Put a 1-inch square of brightly colored plastic tape on the positive axis pole; the tape should contrast with the ball's color to be easily seen. (Use tape on your ball only in practice; tape is not allowed on the surface of a ball used in sanctioned league or tournament play.) Wipe the wax pencil marks off your ball before you begin to bowl again.

Roll your ball consistently down the lane, using a straight ball. Reposition the tape after each shot, until the tape appears motionless (not wobbling) as your ball rolls down the lane. If the tape appears to be motionless, this indicates that the center of the tape square is perfectly positioned over the center of the positive axis pole.

Next, roll 20 balls as consistently as you can, alternating straight balls with hook balls. Note any differences in appearance of the tape as your ball rolls down the lane; the tape should wobble more when you use the hook ball.

Success Goal = alternate 10 straight balls with 10 hook balls

Your Score = (#) _____ total balls

Ball Dynamics
Keys to Success Checklist

In attaining each of the Step 5 Success Goals, you have been introduced to the complex skills necessary to make your ball roll consistently down the lane and knock pins down effectively. If you use the suggested hand positions frequently in well-executed deliveries, your fingers, hand, and wrist will grow stronger, and your ball dynamics will become more effective. However, you will have to practice often to maintain the needed strength for consistent performance. Ask your teacher, coach, or a trained observer to qualitatively evaluate your technique according to the checklist that follows.

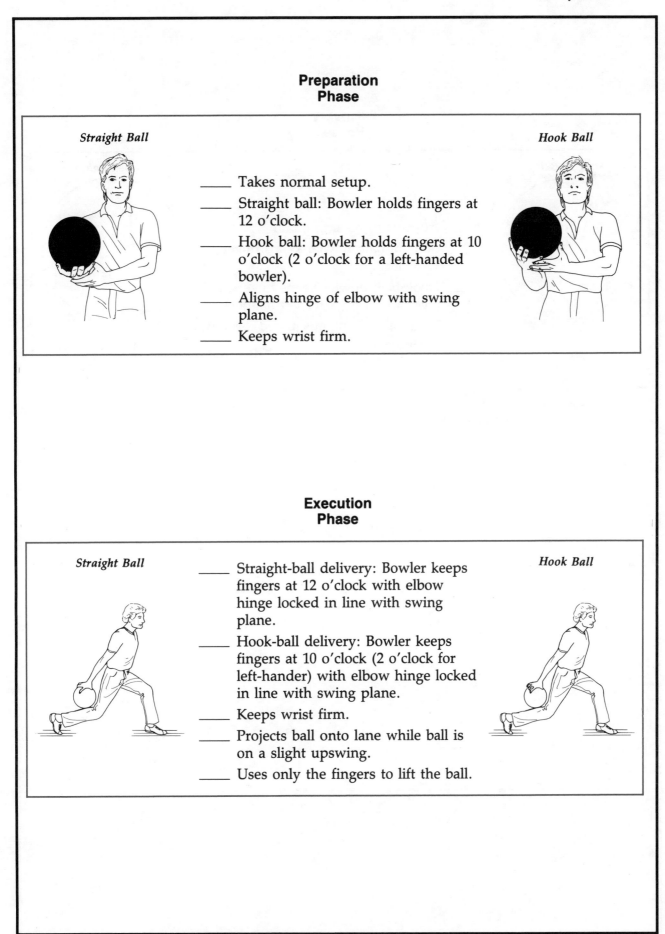

Preparation Phase

Straight Ball

Hook Ball

_____ Takes normal setup.

_____ Straight ball: Bowler holds fingers at 12 o'clock.

_____ Hook ball: Bowler holds fingers at 10 o'clock (2 o'clock for a left-handed bowler).

_____ Aligns hinge of elbow with swing plane.

_____ Keeps wrist firm.

Execution Phase

Straight Ball

Hook Ball

_____ Straight-ball delivery: Bowler keeps fingers at 12 o'clock with elbow hinge locked in line with swing plane.

_____ Hook-ball delivery: Bowler keeps fingers at 10 o'clock (2 o'clock for left-hander) with elbow hinge locked in line with swing plane.

_____ Keeps wrist firm.

_____ Projects ball onto lane while ball is on a slight upswing.

_____ Uses only the fingers to lift the ball.

Recovery
Phase

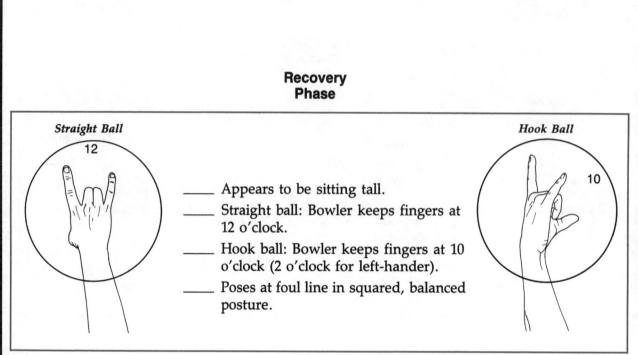

Straight Ball

Hook Ball

____ Appears to be sitting tall.

____ Straight ball: Bowler keeps fingers at 12 o'clock.

____ Hook ball: Bowler keeps fingers at 10 o'clock (2 o'clock for left-hander).

____ Poses at foul line in squared, balanced posture.

Step 6   Strike Targeting

Now you are ready to apply what you have learned about straight and hook balls to making strikes. You obtain strikes by making accurate, well-executed shots toward intelligently selected targets on the lane. A *target* is some mark—a dark spot in a board, a crack between boards, an arrow, or a dot—at which you aim. A *system* is an ordered group of principles, a plan, or a method by which to accomplish something. By consistent use of a *targeting system*, a mindful way to use targets, you can maximize your chances for a strike before you ever actually roll your ball.

In this step you will learn a *target-line system*, which minimizes interference with your swing or your gait to the foul line. First you will learn straight-ball strike targeting because its dynamics limit variability of results at the pins and provide you with more clearcut feedback on the success of your efforts. Then you will learn the slightly more complex skill of hook-ball strike targeting, taking into account the size of your hook when selecting your target line. You will be able to execute your shot comfortably and confidently, using the feel of your shot as feedback to keep yourself executing correctly.

WHY IS STRIKE TARGETING IMPORTANT?

First of all, a targeting system is important because it allows you to be more accurate. Such a system incorporates visual targets, *eye-fixation points*, on the lane that are close to you. It is more difficult to consistently hit a desired point of pin impact 60 feet from the foul line using the pins as a visual target. For this reason, bowlers seriously desiring higher scores usually develop the use of closer targets.

Second, proper use of a targeting system can help you maintain superior execution from shot to shot. If the path you walk bears the proper relationship to your desired ball path, you will be able to swing your ball and walk to the foul line comfortably. If the path does not, you may unconsciously try to force your ball to hit a target for which your body is not aligned, thereby corrupting your swing. If you violate the logical relationship between setup location and target, you will be a chronically inaccurate and frustrated bowler.

A third important point is that if you roll a hook, a targeting system will build control and confidence by helping you *find your line*, locate the best path for your ball to follow, as soon as possible after you start to bowl. If you do not take this precaution, you may assume that the reason for an unexpected ball reaction is poor execution, which most often is not the case. Such an assumption may start a chain of poorly chosen compensations that can destroy your feel for proper execution and, ultimately, your confidence.

Finally, systematic targeting makes you more responsive to changing lane conditions. Even if you find your line quickly and execute well, the lane condition changes as time passes, requiring you to move your target line for your shots to stay in the pocket. If you roll a hook, you must be able to adjust quickly to a changing lane condition, thereby staying in the game, staying competitive. The rule of thumb is this: ''Get in time, get on line, get in the groove, and stay in the groove.''

AIMING METHODS

Four different *alignment*, or aiming, methods are commonly described in bowling texts: there are pin bowling; spot bowling; line bowling; and target-line, or parallel-line, bowling.

Pin bowling is not an effective way of aiming at all. It involves nothing more than standing anywhere on the approach and rolling the ball in the general direction of the rack of pins.

One humorist said, ''You can't improve your aim by shooting at the moon.'' Pin bowling is no more accurate.

Spot bowling, bowling at a spot (any visual target) on the lane surface, provides greater accuracy than pin bowling because the chosen spot is usually closer to the bowler. Because no instruction is usually given concerning a setup location for a given spot, the only definite reference point is the spot itself. Therefore, a bowler is left unguided in picking a place to stand on the approach, increasing the likelihood that a poor choice of a setup location may be made for a given target. The choice may or may not promote a well-coordinated delivery.

Line bowling has been given many different descriptions in bowling texts. None of these descriptions have been adequate, because they refer to as many as five points of reference for a ball path without regard to how these points are to be used as visual targets in the setup and during movement. Further, no advice has been given as to where to stand in relation to a given ball path.

Target-line (parallel-line) bowling is the only true targeting system because it describes a logical relationship between where to look and where to stand during the setup and delivery. Use this system to select a setup location that makes your *approach line* (the path you walk to the foul line) fit your *target line* (the desired ball path). In this way, you will align your swing plane over your target line so that you can execute your delivery comfortably and still project your ball over two necessary points: one at the foul line and one a little farther down the lane at the arrows (see Figure 6.1).

HOW TO EXECUTE STRIKE TARGETING

Strike targeting follows a systematic series of actions, which have been numbered (1

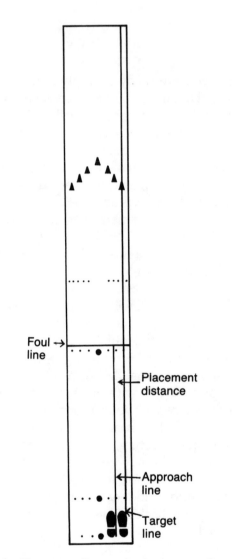

Figure 6.1 Placement distance between target line and approach line.

through 8) on the following pages. The first two actions need to be performed only until you have committed the details to memory. Notice that the remaining actions 3 through 8 are part of a target-line adjustment cycle. You will use this cycle often to make changes in your hook-ball path in response to changing lane conditions. Follow these actions in order.

1. Learn the Lane Targets: The target-line system utilizes certain markers placed on the lane surface. The characteristic arrows and dots are collectively called *Rangefinders®*. (They were developed by the Brunswick Corporation and are illustrated in Figures 6.2a and 6.2b.)

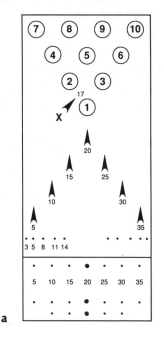

Figure 6.2a Board numbering system for left-handed bowler.

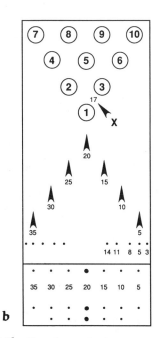

Figure 6.2b Board numbering system for right-handed bowler.

Regardless of which hand you bowl with, you should always recognize lane boards by number. There are 39 boards in a lane, each slightly over 1 inch wide. Identify these boards by counting them from the *outside* (your swingside) channel in the direction of the *inside* (your balance-side) channel. The first of the preceding diagrams illustrates the numbering system to be used by a left-handed bowler; the second diagram illustrates the numbering system to be used by a right-hander. If you are left-handed, count boards from your left to your right; if right-handed, count boards from your right to your left.

The Rangefinder® arrows are placed on every fifth board. Beginning from your outside channel, the first arrow has been placed on board number 5, the second on board number 10, the third on board number 15, and so on; the last arrow is on board number 35. The dots at the foul line are placed on the same board numbers as the arrows, but the small dots 6 feet from the foul line are on board numbers 3, 5, 8, 11, and 14. The approach dots 12 and 15 feet before the foul line, however, are usually placed only on boards 10, 15, 20 (the largest, center dot), 25, and 30.

Here are some examples of arrow and dot relationships:

- The 2nd arrow is outside the 3rd.
- The 2nd arrow is placed on the 10th board from the outside.
- The headpin is centered on board number 20.
- The center arrow is inside with respect to the swingside channel.
- The 1st arrow is on the 5th board.
- The 4th arrow is inside with respect to the 3rd arrow.
- The 5th arrow is located on board number 25.

2. Determine Your Placement Distance: Before you begin learning how to use targets, you must determine the size of your *placement distance* (PD). This measure is the distance in boards between your sliding foot (generally its inside edge) and the point of contact of your ball at or near the foul line (see Figure 6.3).

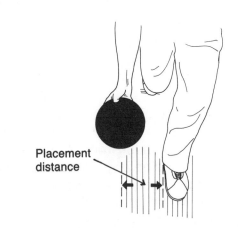

Figure 6.3 Placement distance.

The PD also reflects the horizontal distance between your body's center of gravity and the center of your ball. It is important for you to know this distance so you can determine the appropriate setup location for a particular target line. Large persons with broad shoulders have large placement distances; smaller persons exhibit smaller placement distances. The average PD is 6 to 8 boards. A placement distance will remain constant for the lifetime of any particular bowler whose weight is consistent. Use Drill 2 to determine your own PD.

3. Choose a Target Point: The place where you desire your ball to roll by the arrows is your target point. Let's assume that this target point is your visual target. For now, look at the second arrow from the outside, located on the 10 board (the 10th from the outside channel).

4. Choose Your Ball's Touchdown Point: The point you choose reflects the angle at which you desire to roll your ball over your target point.

For a straight ball, you are temporarily assigned the 8 board as the point at which your ball will touch down, the *touchdown point*. Therefore, your straight-ball target line will be "8 to 10," referring to your two reference points.

For a hook ball, you need to make some adjustments. To straight-ball bowlers, lane conditions are similar from lane to lane. However, to hook-ball bowlers, each lane has a distinct *hook power*, or tendency for a ball to hook. Therefore, you must roll one or more balls to

see how much your ball hooks before you can know where your ball should touch down to strike while you use a given target point. For now, you are assigned a preliminary line, or *test target line*, of 10 to 10. You will be rolling your test balls straight down the 10th board from the outside channel, "down ten." Later (in Drill 4), you will get a chance to sharpen your skills at adjusting your target line (at *playing lanes*) with the hook ball.

5. Project an Imaginary Extension: Visualize an extension of your target line back to the area of the approach at which you take your setup.

For a straight ball, because you stand about the same distance from the foul line as the second arrow is from the foul line, you may assume that the imaginary target line extension crosses your setup area at about the sixth board ($10 - 8 = 2$, $8 - 2 = 6$) (see Figure 6.4).

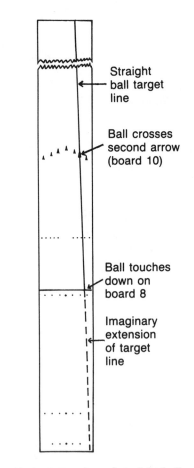

Straight ball target line

Ball crosses second arrow (board 10)

Ball touches down on board 8

Imaginary extension of target line

Figure 6.4 Imaginary extension of straight-ball target line.

With a hook ball, say your preliminary target line is 10 to 10. Then your extended target line would cross your setup area at board 10 (see Figure 6.5).

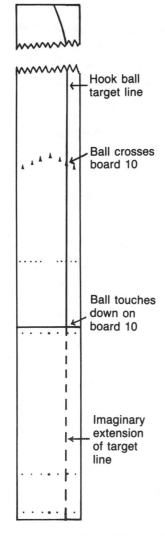

Figure 6.5   Imaginary extension of hook-ball target line.

6. Take Your Setup at the Appropriate Location With Respect to Your Target Line: Position both feet so that they are parallel with each other and with your target line.

Using a straight ball now, to find the setup point for the inside of your sliding foot sole, simply add your placement distance to the number 6. Let's assume that your placement distance is 7; therefore, 6 + 7 gives you a setup location of the 13 board.

When you deliver a straight ball, your intended approach line now begins on board 13 at your setup location and ends on board 10 at the foul line. Place the edge of your sliding foot on the edge of board 13 so that the board is completely visible to the inside of your foot.

For your test target line for a hook ball, adding a hypothetical placement distance (PD) of 7 boards gives you a setup location of 17. Your intended approach line begins on board 17 at your setup location and ends on board 17 at the foul line. Place the edge of your sliding foot on the edge of board 17 so that the board is completely visible to the arch side of your foot (see Figure 6.6).

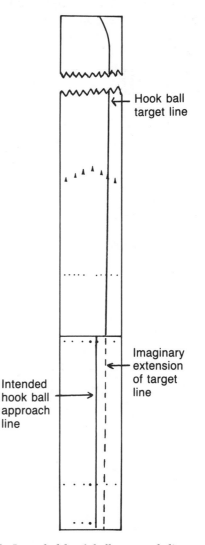

Figure 6.6   Intended hook-ball approach line.

7. Fix Your Eyes on Your Visual Target:
Keeping your eyes fixed on a well-defined visual target is valuable in stabilizing your head, neck, and back to keep them from moving during your delivery (see Figure 6.7). Further, the act of fixing your gaze on a visual target draws your body toward the target during your approach. Your visual target may not be the same as your target point; you may have to look at a visual target to the inside or outside of the target point in order to roll your ball over the target point itself.

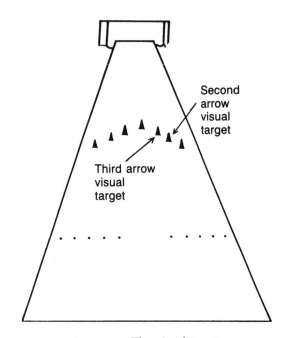

Figure 6.7 The visual target.

8. Execute Your Shot Properly: Note the board number where your ball rolled by the arrows. Also note the board number upon which your foot stopped in your slide. Get into the habit of considering both boards in evaluating the quality of your execution. Take the following courses of action (do not be concerned if you do not make strikes—you are determining accuracy, not pinfall average):

- If you executed properly, if your ball passed over the correct board at the arrows, and if it went on to contact the pins at the strike pocket (at the 17th board from the outside channel), roll another properly executed shot along the same target line.
- If you did not execute properly, regardless of whether your ball passed over the correct board at the arrows or contacted the pins at the strike pocket, do not make any adjustments to your target line until you have corrected your execution.
- If you executed properly and your ball passed over the correct board at the arrows, but did not contact the pins at the strike pocket, verify the correctness of—and make adjustments to—your target line by repeating actions 4 through 8.

Effective strike targeting using the target-line system is nothing more than becoming skilled at carrying out the mental checklist illustrated in Figure 6.8). For more information on strike targeting, see Allen and Ritger (1981).

Figure 6.8 Keys to Success: Strike Targeting

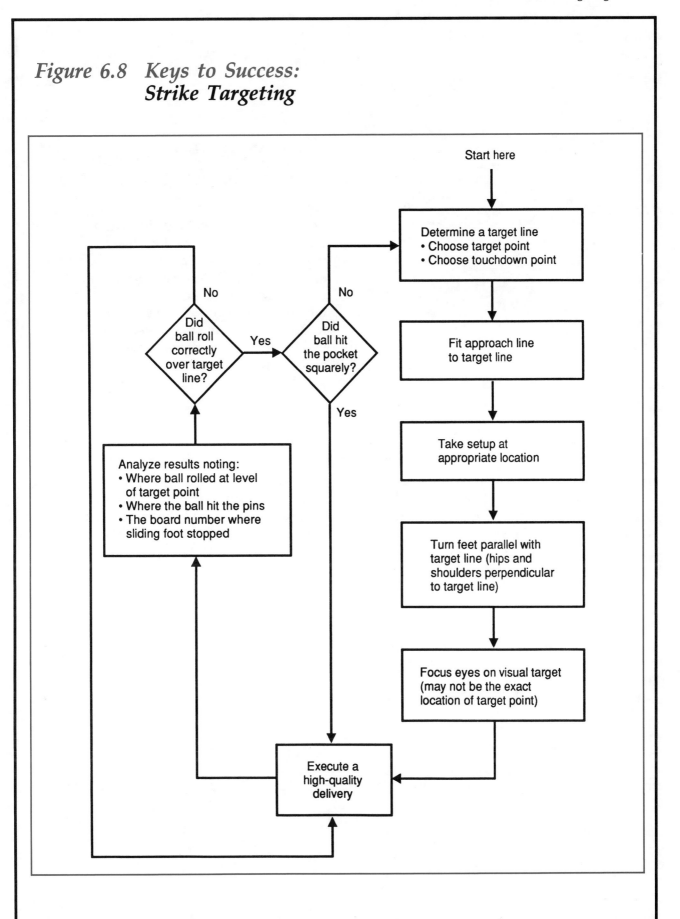

Detecting Straight-Ball Strike-Targeting Errors

Your straight-ball strike delivery should proceed along a path from your hand, over the target point, and straight to the strike pocket at the 17th board. You can increase the consistency with which you roll your straight ball into the strike pocket if you learn how to recognize errors in straight-ball strike targeting. Some common errors and suggestions on how to correct them follow.

ERROR

CORRECTION

1. Ball misses target to the inside and hits too *high* on the headpin, or it completely misses the headpin to the inside.

1. Make sure that you execute properly and that your swing is in line with your shoulder and the target. Also make sure that you do not look to the inside of the target.

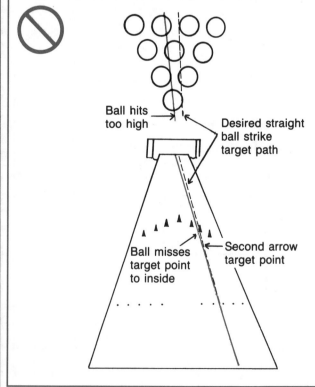

Ball hits too high

Desired straight ball strike target path

Ball misses target point to inside

Second arrow target point

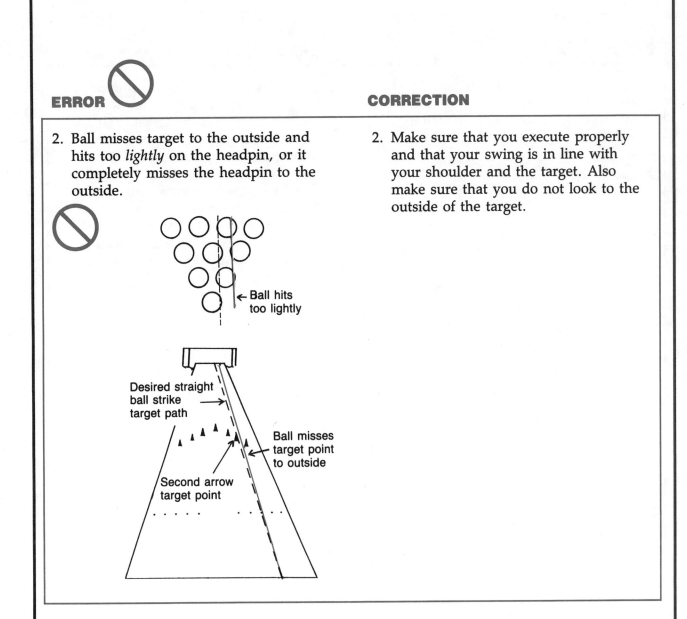

ERROR

ERROR

CORRECTION

2. Ball misses target to the outside and hits too *lightly* on the headpin, or it completely misses the headpin to the outside.

2. Make sure that you execute properly and that your swing is in line with your shoulder and the target. Also make sure that you do not look to the outside of the target.

← Ball hits too lightly

Desired straight ball strike target path →

Ball misses target point to outside

Second arrow target point

ERROR ⊘

CORRECTION

3. Ball consistently hits the target but misses the desired point of impact at the pins to the same degree each time.

⊘

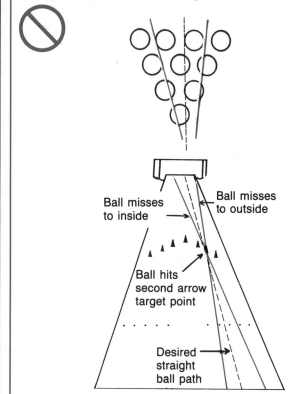

Ball misses to inside

Ball misses to outside

Ball hits second arrow target point

Desired straight ball path

3. Make sure that you execute properly and that your swing is in line with your shoulder and the target. You are probably not properly aligned with your target. Move your feet in the same direction as the impact error; if your ball is missing to the outside of the pocket, move your setup location to the outside; if missing to the inside, move to the inside. You may need to recompute your placement distance.

4. Ball consistently misses target to the same degree.

⊘

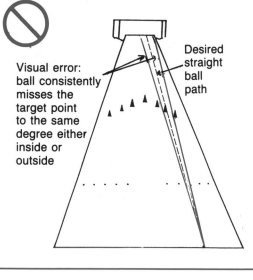

Visual error: ball consistently misses the target point to the same degree either inside or outside

Desired straight ball path

4. Make sure that you execute properly and that your swing is in line with your shoulder and the target. You may have a visual error that must be compensated for. Move your gaze in the direction opposite your error until your ball is consistently rolling over your chosen target point. Note: You may always have to look at a visual target that is to one side of your intended target point to compensate for a vision problem. Experimentation is often necessary.

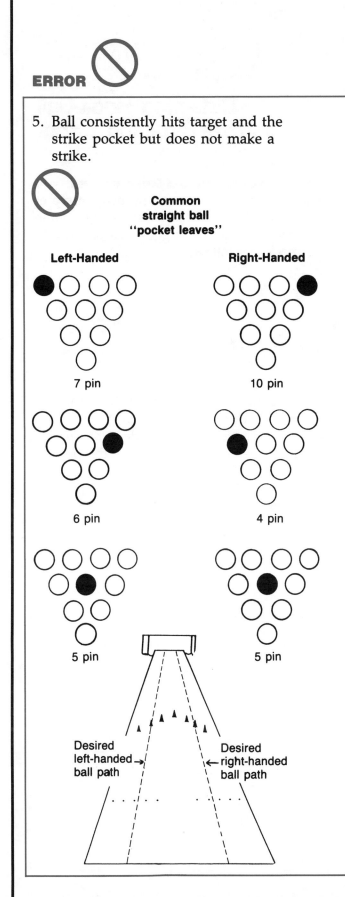

ERROR

CORRECTION

5. Ball consistently hits target and the strike pocket but does not make a strike.

5. Make sure that you execute properly and that your swing is in line with your shoulder and the target. Make half-board adjustments to your setup location until your ball is hitting the pocket in the proper way to carry the pins. Always remember the exact location to which you move your feet.

Detecting Hook-Ball Strike-Targeting Errors

Your hook-ball strike delivery should proceed straight along a path from your hand, over your target point, and to the break point. From the break point, the ball should move toward the strike pocket at the 17th board. You can increase the consistency with which you roll your hook ball into the strike pocket if you learn how to recognize and properly interpret errors in hook-ball strike targeting. Some common errors and suggestions on how to correct them follow.

ERROR

CORRECTION

1. Ball hits target point but misses the strike pocket to the inside, hitting the headpin too full (too high) or missing it altogether on the inside.

1. Try again with proper execution and the correct visual target. If the second attempt does not work, move your setup location to the inside, 2 boards at a time, until your ball hits the pins at the strike pocket.

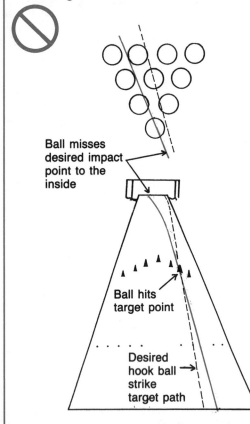

Ball misses desired impact point to the inside

Ball hits target point

Desired hook ball strike target path

ERROR   **CORRECTION**

2. Ball hits target point but misses the strike pocket to the outside, hitting the headpin too lightly or missing it altogether.

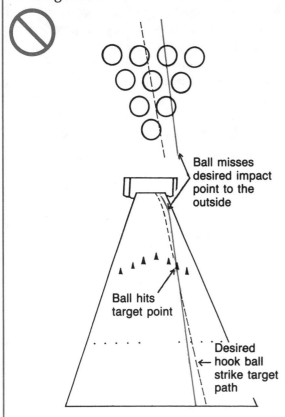

Ball misses desired impact point to the outside

Ball hits target point

Desired hook ball strike target path

2. Try again with proper execution and the correct visual target. If the second attempt does not work, move your setup location to the outside, 2 boards at a time, until your ball hits the pins at the strike pocket.

3. Ball consistently misses target point.

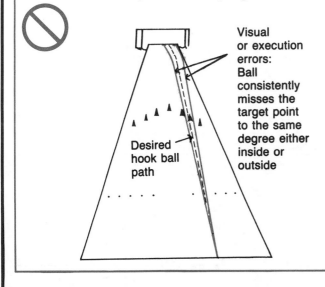

Visual or execution errors: Ball consistently misses the target point to the same degree either inside or outside

Desired hook ball path

3. Make sure that you are executing properly and that you are using the proper visual target. Also, see Straight-Ball Correction 4.

ERROR

CORRECTION

4. Ball consistently hits target and the strike pocket but does not strike consistently.

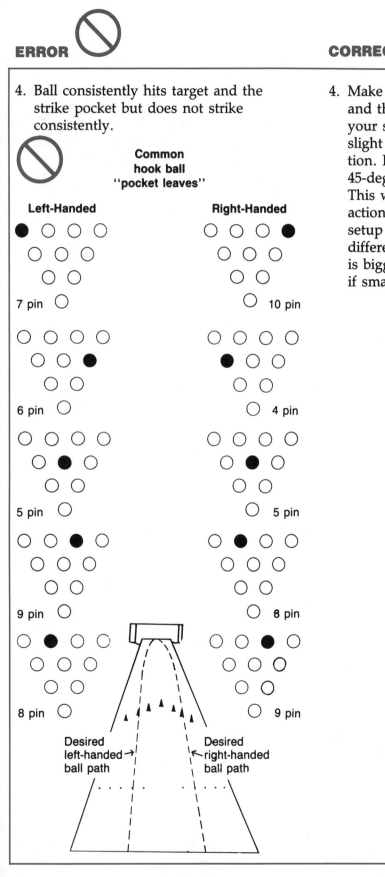

Common hook ball "pocket leaves"

4. Make sure that you execute properly and that your swing is in line with your shoulder and the target. Make slight adjustments in your finger position. For example, change from the 45-degree to a 30- or 60-degree position. This will create a different ball reaction. You may have to move your setup location in response to the different amount of hook. If your hook is bigger, move your feet to the inside; if smaller, move your feet outside.

Strike-Targeting Drills

1. *Targeting Quiz*

Study the figures that show the location of the pins, dots, and arrows. In addition, study the following figure, which shows the lengths of bowling lane segments. When you feel ready, close the book and have your practice partner ask you the following questions, scoring your responses.

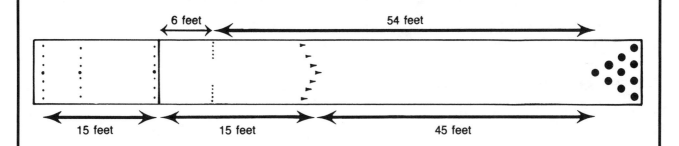

Target Marker Quiz

a. Name, in the following order, the board numbers upon which are set the following pins (10 responses):

    1 pin, 7 pin, 10 pin, 5 pin, 8 pin,
    9 pin, 2 pin, 3 pin, 4 pin, and 6 pin

b. Name the board numbers upon which are placed the target arrows, from the outside to the inside (7 responses).

c. Name the board numbers upon which are placed the dots at the foul line, from the outside to the inside (7 responses).

d. How far are the two sets of approach dots from the foul line (2 responses)?

e. How far is the foul line from the headpin? The arrows from the foul line? The arrows from the headpin? The small set of lane dots from the foul line? (Four responses; all may be approximate.)

f. Name the board numbers upon which lie the small set of lane dots, from the outside to the inside (5 responses).

Success Goal = 35 out of 35 correct answers

Your Score = (#) _____ correct answers

Answer Key to Target Marker Quiz

a. Right-handed: 20, 35, 5, 20, 25, 15, 25, 15, 30, 10
    Left-handed: 20, 5, 35, 20, 15, 25, 15, 25, 10, 30

(Answers b. through f. apply to both right- and left-handed bowlers.)

b. 5, 10, 15, 20, 25, 30, 35

c. 5, 10, 15, 20, 25, 30, 35

d. 12 feet and 15 feet

e. 60 feet, 15 feet, 45 feet, 6 feet

f. 3, 5, 8, 11, 14

2. *Placement Distance Determination*

It is usually necessary to determine your personal placement distance (PD) only once. You may need to repeat the determination if your weight fluctuates greatly, though.

Take a sitting-tall finish position with your ball dangling to your swingside. Make sure that your balance arm is correctly positioned and your shoulders are level with the approach. ''Sit down'' even more, so that your ball touches the approach; keep your back upright. Keep your swingside leg behind you so that you must balance on your sliding foot, keeping it directly under your center of gravity.

Have your partner use a ruler to measure the distance between the inner edge of your sliding foot and the point of contact of your ball. Make 5 measurements in inches, recording them in the Success Goal Section. Take the average as your PD and translate inches to boards by dividing the PD in inches by 1.1.

Use the PD in boards in all of your subsequent bowling alignment procedures in the rest of the lessons in this book, as well as for all of your future bowling activities.

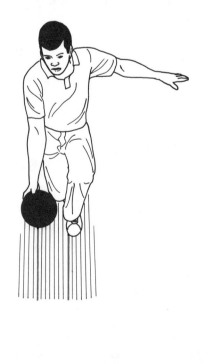

Success Goal = determine personal PD in boards after 5 measurements

	Measurement					
	1	2	3	4	5	Total
PD (inches)	_____	_____	_____	_____	_____	_____

Average = Total/5 = _____; PD in boards = Average ÷ 1.1 = _____

Your Score = (#) _____ boards PD

3. *Straight-Ball Strike Targeting*

It is now time for you to roll a trial game consisting of 10 scored first-ball deliveries. You will use a straight ball and a target line of 8 to 10.

Your partner will use a scoresheet to record execution information, but not score pinfall or second-ball attempts. After your game has begun, do not talk to your partner except as you will be directed. Prepare your scoresheet following the example of Sample Scoresheet 1.

Sample Scoresheet 1

NAME HDCP	1	2	3	4	5	6	7	8	9	10
1 SETUP LOCATION										
2 SLIDE LOCATION										
3 TARGET AREA BOARD										
4 IMPACT BOARD										

Take your setup on the same board every time; tell your partner what this board number is before you start so that it can be entered in all 10 frames of the first game line as the "setup location." After each delivery, look down at your sliding toe, noting the number of the first board that is completely visible just to the inside of your sliding foot. Tell your partner this board number so that it can be recorded as "slide location" in the proper frame of the second game line.

Your partner must watch your ball's reaction—not your form—to gather the rest of the information. Therefore, while you are in your setup, your partner should begin to gaze at the second arrow, your intended target. As your ball rolls down the lane, your partner should note and record in the appropriate frames of your prepared scoresheet (a) the board number over which the ball rolled near the arrows (the *target area board*) and (b) the board number

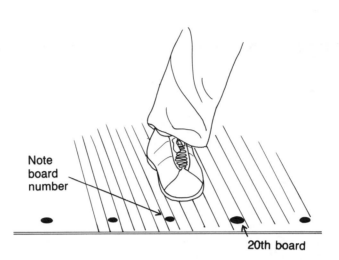

over which the ball rolled when it hit the pins (the *impact board*). Both board numbers should be immediately recorded in the appropriate frames of your scoresheet.

Your partner should give you 1 check mark (point) for each time an entry matches the ideal (not including setup location). The ideals for the entries should be:

Slide location = board 8 + your PD = _____

Target area = board 10

Impact board = board 17

Success Goal = complete 3 trial games rating the following characteristics

	Characteristic	Trial game 1	Trial game 2	Trial game 3
Your Score =	Slide location	_____	_____	_____
	Target area	_____	_____	_____
	Impact point	_____	_____	_____
	Total points	_____	_____	_____

Performance Evaluation

When you have finished, discuss your performance with your partner. Use the following criteria.

a. If the numbers listed in the "Slide location" row seem to be consistent—not varying more than one board—you are probably executing your delivery well.

b. If the numbers listed in the "Target area" row consistently read "10," congratulations! If they do not, review the "Detecting Straight-Ball Strike-Targeting Errors" section earlier in this step.

c. If the numbers listed in the "Impact point" row consistently read "17," congratulations! If not, follow Straight-Ball Correction 3 directions.

4. Hook-Ball Strike Targeting

You may now use the targeting system to align your body for striking with your hook ball on the available lane condition. Always remember that you must walk parallel with your target line for consistency in hitting the strike pocket. Disregard the fact that you may be walking at an angle to the foul line and that you may be walking away from the pocket when rolling your hook ball.

You will bowl a trial game consisting of 10 first balls. Your partner will act as observer to tell you whether you actually roll your ball over your attempted target line. Take a warm-up first, rolling your ball along a 10 to 10 target line to develop proper execution. Your partner will use two game lines on a scoresheet to record execution information, but not pinfall or second-ball attempts. Prepare a scoresheet, using Sample Scoresheet 2 as a model.

Sample Scoresheet 2

NAME HDCP	1	2	3	4	5	6	7	8	9	10
1 TARGET LINE	10 / 10									
2 IMPACT POINT										

Before you roll your first ball of each frame of game one, declare your intended target line so your observer can record it and later give you feedback with respect to your accuracy.

After each of your first-ball attempts, your observer should indicate "yes" if you hit the target line, or "no" if you did not. You should also analyze how your delivery felt; be honest with yourself!

After your successful attempt, your partner should enter in the appropriate frame of the second game line the board number where your ball rolled as it hit the pins. Then your partner records in the next frame of the first game line the target line that you will next attempt to roll your ball over. Upon hitting it successfully with good execution, your partner should record the results at impact in the second frame of the second game line.

Note: You may have to attempt the first ball of each frame more than once to hit the designated target line and to make sure that you executed properly before your partner can make any entry in a game line, moving your setup location as explained in Hook Ball Corrections 1 and 2.

Repeat these procedures until you find the proper target line for hitting the pocket, the 17th board. Then attempt to hit the pocket 4 times in a row before you run out of frames in the trial game. Regardless of the number of consecutive "17" entries in a trial game, move on to the next trial game after 10 frames. You may stop as soon as you have obtained four pocket hits in a row within a trial game or when you have completed 3 trial games (30 total balls), whichever occurs first.

Success Goal = 4 pocket hits in a row within a single trial game, or completion of 3 trial games

Trial games

	1	2	3
Your Score = (#)	_____	_____	_____

Strike-Targeting
Keys to Success Checklist

Naturally, the success of a targeting system depends on how well you execute your movements. To check on your ability to use targets properly, ask your teacher, coach, or a trained observer to qualitatively evaluate your technique according to the checklist below. Because this is a mental checklist, you need to verbally declare your choices and activities to your observer during your evaluation.

Planning and Preparation
Phase

_____ Declares a target point (in this case, the second arrow).

_____ Declares a target line (includes touchdown point and target point).

_____ Declares an approach line to fit the target line (takes into account the extended imaginary target line and the PD).

_____ Takes a setup in the appropriate location.

_____ Turns both feet parallel to target line.

_____ Remains still, apparently looking at visual target.

Execution
Phase

_____ Executes a high-quality delivery.

Analysis
of Results

_____ Declares board number where the sliding foot stopped at the foul line.

_____ Declares board number where the ball hit the pins.

_____ Declares board number where the ball actually rolled at the level of the target.

Repetition
or Adjustment

_____ If target line is successful, bowler declares that the next option is to repeat proper execution on same target line.

_____ If target line is not successful, bowler declares that the next option is to select another target line.

Step 7 **Refine Pendulum Swing and Takeaway**

In the delivery, the takeaway is the movement of the balance arm from a position of supporting the ball in the fully extended pushaway to a position out from the body, slightly down, and toward the back. The balance arm is held in this position throughout the delivery until the swing arm completes the follow-through. Coordinating these two elements establishes the one-piece nature of the overall, combined movement.

WHY IS THE COORDINATED PENDULUM SWING AND TAKEAWAY IMPORTANT?

When the balance arm is taken away in synchrony with the fall of the ball into the swing and is held in the proper position, it counterbalances some of the weight of the ball. More importantly, the balance arm stabilizes the pivot for the swing. Thus, an imaginary line running from the swing shoulder through the other shoulder and to the balance hand may be pictured as an axis around which the swing rotates. In keeping your swing shoulder from dropping too low and both shoulders from rotating, your balance arm—if carefully timed, placed, and held in the proper position—helps to ensure against misdirected shots. Otherwise, rotating shoulders allows your swing to deviate from the ideal swing plane, causing a bumpout, a wraparound, or a combination of both called a *looped swing*.

Detecting Errors in the Coordinated Pendulum Swing and Takeaway

You can markedly increase your accuracy if you learn how to recognize errors in the coordinated pendulum swing and takeaway and in the position of your balance arm. Some common pendulum swing and takeaway errors and suggestions on how to correct them are now presented.

ERROR ⃠	CORRECTION
1. You take away your balance hand too early.	1. Wait until the count of "one" to begin your takeaway.
2. You take away your balance hand too late.	2. Begin your takeaway just as your ball begins its fall into the swing.
3. Your balance arm moves to the wrong position during the takeaway.	3. After the count of "one," say to yourself, "Point to the wall," and move your balance arm crisply to the out, down, and back position.

Coordinated Pendulum Swing and Takeaway Drills

1. Assisted Takeaway Coordination

Assume the extension setup position with your partner supporting the weight of the ball. This time, place your balance hand underneath your bowling hand. Stand erect in preparation for the ball to fall into the swing.

Count your swing cadence to yourself in order to get ready. When you feel ready to allow the ball to swing, say, "one." Upon hearing you say this, your partner, continuing to count for you, should let the ball fall into the swing.

As your ball begins its fall, execute the takeaway—remember to point your balance arm out, down, and back—as if to the wall. Close your eyes and study the relationship of timing between the ball falling into the swing and your balance arm moving into its proper position. Your balance hand should be in its final position on your partner's count of "two" and should remain outstretched in this position during the counts of "three" (top of the backswing) and "four" (passing the swingside leg during the forward swing).

Success Goal = 10 consecutive coordinated swings and takeaways

Your Score = (#) _____ consecutive coordinated swings and takeaways

2. High and Low Takeaway Awareness

This drill shows you how two improper takeaway positions feel, better preparing you for correcting such errors quickly. You and your partner set up as before. Now, however, deliberately change your takeaway position to an incorrect one and ask yourself whether you feel more or less stable and whether your shoulders feel uneven.

a. *Feeling a high takeaway*. When the ball begins to go into the downswing at the count of ''one,'' move your balance hand to a position approximately 1 foot higher than the level of its shoulder. Concentrate on the effects of this error on the position of your swingside shoulder. Alternate with correct takeaways to sense the differences.

b. *Feeling a low takeaway*. When the ball begins to go into the downswing at the count of ''one,'' move your balance hand directly to your balance side, with your hand almost touching the side of your upper leg. Concentrate on the effects of this error on the position of your swingside shoulder. Alternate with correct takeaways to sense the differences.

Success Goal =

a. compare 5 high with 5 correct takeaways and swings

b. compare 5 low with 5 correct takeaways and swings

Your Score =

a. (#) _____ comparisons high with correct takeaways and swings

b. (#) _____ comparisons low with correct takeaways and swings

3. Front and Back Takeaway Awareness

As with the previous drill, the objective here is to deliberately deviate from the correct takeaway position so you can study how the errors feel.

a. *Feeling a front takeaway.* When the ball begins to go into the downswing at the count of "one," move your balance hand to a position in front of its shoulder, as if you were reaching for something. Concentrate on the effects of this error on the position of your swingside shoulder. Alternate with correct takeaways to sense the differences.

b. *Feeling a back takeaway.* When the ball begins to go into the downswing at the count of "one," move your balance hand to a position directly behind the hip of the sliding leg. Concentrate on the effects of this error on the position of your swingside shoulder during the swing. Alternate with correct takeaways to sense the differences.

Success Goal =

   a. compare 5 front with 5 correct takeaways and swings

   b. compare 5 back with 5 correct takeaways and swings

Your Score =

   a. (#) _____ comparisons of front with correct takeaways and swings

   b. (#) _____ comparisons of back with correct takeaways and swings

4. 300 Drill

This drill involves scoring a game without actually counting the pins knocked down. Ask your partner to evaluate your ability to incorporate the coordinated pendulum swing and takeaway into your delivery.

  Be sure to use proper strike-targeting techniques on every ball. Don't worry about picking up spares, just concentrate on using the skills you've already learned.

  If you execute correctly on your first ball, mark a strike on your scoresheet. If you do not execute correctly on your first ball, mark 9 points. If you execute correctly on your second ball, mark a spare. If you do not execute correctly on your second ball, mark a miss. Tally your points to get as close as possible to a perfect ''300'' game.

Success Goal = 225 out of 300 possible points

Your Score = (#) _____ points

Step 8 Refine Your Pushaway

The proper technique for the pushaway is the act of pushing the ball with both hands into the desired plane of the swing at a predetermined height, in line with the swing shoulder and a desired visual fixation point.

Seeing where your ball is at the end of your pushaway is as important as attaining the feel of a proper pushaway, because of the need to accurately push away the ball in line with a target. After completing the drills in this step, you will gain an understanding of undesirable pushaway positions and attain a clearer idea of the role of the balance hand during the pushaway.

WHY IS THE PUSHAWAY IMPORTANT?

A properly executed pushaway promotes a free-pendulum swing, with more natural (unforced) ball speed. A ball placed reasonably high into the swing represents more potential energy; a ball placed lower represents less. The lower your pushaway is, the lower your backswing (if you do not hoist the ball) and the shorter your total swing time. The higher your pushaway is, the higher your backswing (if you do not clip the backswing) and the longer your total swing time.

A well-executed pushaway also promotes accuracy by keeping your swing plane in line with your intended visual fixation point, or *visual target*. As you learned in Step 2, a misaligned swing tends to pull you off balance; more effort is then needed to maintain control of your center of gravity. If you direct your pushaway too close to the front center of your body, you have to counteract this imbalance with a step to the outside. If your pushaway is directed too far to the outside, you have to compensate by stepping to the inside.

Detecting Pushaway Errors

Unless the pushaway is carefully positioned into the swing plane, errors may occur in the direction of the ball when it goes down the lane. Seemingly small errors in the pushaway can result in large errors by the time the ball reaches the point of impact with the pins.

You can increase your accuracy if you learn how to recognize errors in the pushaway. Some common pushaway errors and suggestions on how to correct them follow.

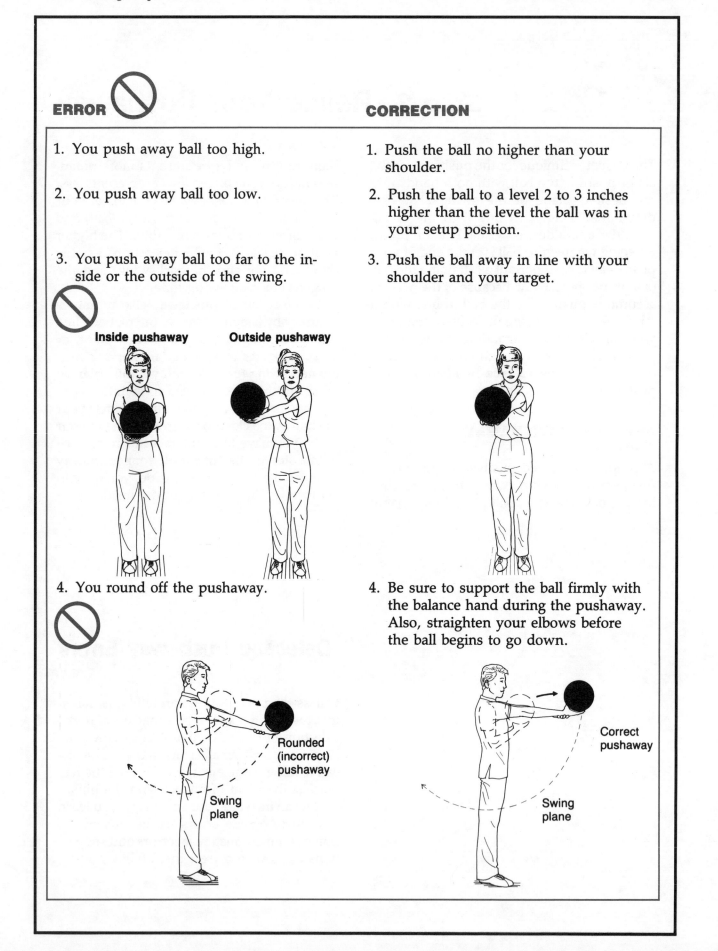

ERROR 🚫

CORRECTION

1. You push away ball too high.

2. You push away ball too low.

3. You push away ball too far to the inside or the outside of the swing.

1. Push the ball no higher than your shoulder.

2. Push the ball to a level 2 to 3 inches higher than the level the ball was in your setup position.

3. Push the ball away in line with your shoulder and your target.

Inside pushaway   Outside pushaway

4. You round off the pushaway.

4. Be sure to support the ball firmly with the balance hand during the pushaway. Also, straighten your elbows before the ball begins to go down.

Rounded (incorrect) pushaway

Swing plane

Correct pushaway

Swing plane

Pushaway Drills

1. Pushaway Placement and Coordination

Assume the normal setup position and work with a partner face-to-face. Your partner should be ready for you to place your ball into his or her hands at the proper time in your pushaway. Your partner's hands, held 2 to 3 inches higher than your ball in the setup position, represent your *pushaway destination*.

   You should begin counting the cadence aloud. On your count of ''four,'' be ready to push the ball with both hands, with the weight carried by the balance hand, so that it arrives into your partner's waiting hands on ''one.'' When you push your ball into your partner's hands, be gentle! Do not close your eyes and do not take any steps! In order to lessen the chance for a muscled swing, use your balance hand to carry the weight of the ball to the fully extended (elbows straight) position. Focus your attention on the stability of your back and shoulders and on the relatively relaxed state of your bowling arm.

Success Goal = 20 correctly timed pushaways

Your Score = (#) _____ correctly timed pushaways

2. *High and Low Pushaway Awareness*

This drill and the following one illustrate common pushaway errors so you can correct such errors quickly when they occur. Set up for each of the following exercises exactly as you did in the first drill, with your partner assisting you as before. Now, however, deliberately change your pushaway destination to an incorrect one so you can study how the error looks and feels. In each case, ask yourself whether you feel strained, stooped, or less stable. Note whether you think you could perform each type of pushaway consistently.

a. *Feeling an excessively high pushaway.* Have your partner hold waiting hands 1 to 2 feet higher than in the first drill. At the count of ''four'' in your cadence (see Drill 1), begin to push the ball away to this higher destination. Repeat this type of pushaway 5 times, alternating with 5 correct pushaways, noting the comparative effects of this error.

b. *Feeling an excessively low pushaway.* Have your partner hold waiting hands 1 to 2 feet lower than in the first drill, so that the pushaway destination will be at a level between 2 to 3 feet from the approach. At the proper time, push the ball away to this destination. Repeat this type of pushaway 5 times, alternating with 5 correct pushaways, noting the comparative effects of this error.

High pushaway

Low pushaway

Success Goal =

   a. compare 5 high with 5 correct pushaways

   b. compare 5 low with 5 correct pushaways

Your Score =

   a. (#) _____ comparisons of high with correct pushaways

   b. (#) _____ comparisons of low with correct pushaways

3. Inside and Outside Pushaway Awareness

One of the most persistent and unnoticed errors is that of pushing the ball away to the inside or the outside of the intended swing plane. Small deviations from the ideal here can mean missing the desired point of pin impact by a large margin.

a. *Inside (convergent) pushaway.* Have your partner hold waiting hands 6 to 8 inches farther to the inside than in the first drill. At the proper time, push the ball away to this more inside destination. Repeat this movement 5 times, alternating with 5 correct pushaways, noting the comparative effects of this error. Note the feeling of being cramped with the ball moving somewhat across your body, and the feeling of being out of balance.

b. *Outside (divergent) pushaway.* Have your partner hold waiting hands 6 to 8 inches farther to the outside than the ideal pushaway destination. At the proper time, push the ball away to this more outside destination. Repeat this movement 5 times, alternating with 5 correct pushaways, noting the comparative effects of this error. Note the feeling of being loose or off balance to the outside with the ball moving somewhat away from your body.

Success Goal =

   a. compare 5 inside with 5 correct pushaways

   b. compare 5 outside with 5 correct pushaways

Your Score =

   a. (#) _____ comparisons of inside with correct pushaways

   b. (#) _____ comparisons of outside with correct pushaways

4. 300 Drill

This drill involves scoring a game without actually counting the pins knocked down. Ask your partner to evaluate your ability to incorporate the pushaway into your delivery.

   Be sure to use proper strike-targeting techniques on every ball. Don't worry about picking up spares, just concentrate on using the skills you've learned so far.

   If you execute correctly on your first ball, mark a strike on your scoresheet. If you do not execute correctly on your first ball, mark 8 points. If you execute correctly on your second ball, mark a spare. If you do not execute correctly on your second ball, mark a miss. Tally your points to get as close as possible to a perfect "300" game.

Success Goal = 225 out of 300 possible points

Your Score = (#) _____ points

Step 9 **Refine Three Skills**

You have separately linked three basic skills to your cadence—the pendulum swing, takeaway, and pushaway. Now all you have to do is check that you are fluidly combining these three skills in rhythm with your cadence.

WHY IS THE COORDINATED PUSHAWAY, PENDULUM SWING, AND TAKEAWAY IMPORTANT?

The pendulum swing and the takeaway begin the instant the pushaway ends. It is vital that you integrate the movements of your upper body into a smooth, rhythmic sequence, and that the feel of this coordinated movement is ingrained. By integrating these upper-body movements, you will avoid making execution errors that can lower your bowling scores.

Pushaway/Pendulum Swing/Takeaway Coordination Drills

1. Upper Body Coordination

This is a solo drill. Assume a normal setup position. Tense the muscles of your spine in preparation for the pushaway. Count your swing cadence to yourself before making any movement.

Push your ball to the extended pushaway destination and say ''one.'' As the ball begins to fall from the extended pushaway position, execute the takeaway by moving your balance hand to the ideal out, down, and back position. Say ''two'' as the ball reaches the bottom of your swing. Say ''three'' as the ball reaches the top of the backswing.

Allow your ball to begin its forward swing drawn only by the force of gravity. Say ''four'' as your ball once again passes your swingside leg at the bottom of your forward swing. On the count of ''four,'' begin to move your balance hand so that it will meet the ball returning to the original extension position from which it fell into the swing. With your balance hand underneath the ball, return to the normal setup position at rest, in preparation for repeating the drill.

Alternate doing the drills with your eyes open and closed; concentrate on the timing relationship among the three elements. Feel your elbows lock, the ball falling into the swing, and your balance arm moving crisply to the desired position.

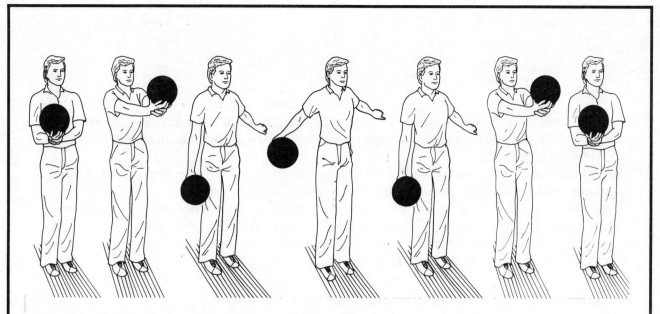

Success Goal = 5 consecutive coordinated swings

3 with eyes open

2 with eyes closed

Your Score =

(#) _____ swings with eyes open

(#) _____ swings with eyes closed

2. Assisted Troubleshooting

Repeat the sequence of movements you just did. This time your partner will help you evaluate your form. Have your partner observe and evaluate one of the Success Goal characteristics each time you do the sequence. If you do not perform a characteristic well, repeat Drill 1 alone and unobserved, focusing your attention on refining that characteristic until you feel ready for your partner's evaluation assistance in performing Drill 2 again.

Success Goal = all 5 movements done correctly

Characteristic	Yes	No
Back is straight	_____	_____
Pushaway square to shoulder	_____	_____
Pushaway slightly up, not rounded	_____	_____
Takeaway timed with fall of ball	_____	_____
Balance arm held outstretched	_____	_____

Your Score = (#) _____ ''yes'' responses

3. 300 Drill

This drill involves scoring a game without actually counting the pins knocked down. Ask your partner to evaluate your ability to incorporate the pushaway, pendulum swing, and take-away into your delivery.

Be sure to use proper strike-targeting technique on every ball. Don't worry about picking up spares, just concentrate on using the skills you've already learned.

If you execute correctly on your first ball, mark a strike on your scoresheet. If you do not execute correctly on your first ball, mark 7 points. If you execute correctly on your second ball, mark a spare. If you do not execute correctly on your second ball, mark a miss. Tally your points to get as close as possible to a perfect ''300'' game.

Success Goal = 225 out of 300 possible points

Your Score = (#) _____ points

Step 10 Refine First Step and Pushaway

You will now integrate the first movement of your lower body (your first footstep) with your pushaway. You will again use your cadence as a tool to link multiple movements into one coordinated movement.

WHY IS IT IMPORTANT TO COORDINATE THE FIRST STEP WITH THE PUSHAWAY?

Proper timing of the pushaway with the swingside foot in the first step is necessary to create a free-pendulum swing. Coordination of the pushaway with the first step involves getting the elbows extended at the very instant the swingside heel touches down in the first step. A "heel-down, sole-up" first step position is preferred because it helps you keep your shoulders back and your back upright—very important in controlling your center of gravity.

In the actual delivery, a late pushaway can cause your ball to arrive later than the sliding foot at the foul line. A late pushaway can also cause you to miss your target to either side, to drop your ball before the desired release point, or to *pull* your ball, imparting excessive lift with the fingers at the release.

An early pushaway in a full approach can cause your ball to arrive at the foul line before your sliding foot. An early pushaway can also cause you to *hop*—actually, to take a quick step—between the second and third steps in the four-step delivery, as well as cause a loss of lift with your fingers at the release. An early pushaway can also cause your ball to be late at the foul line if your upper body leans forward as your ball begins to fall into the downswing.

Detecting Errors in the Coordinated First Step and Pushaway

You can increase your ability to maintain proper coordination between your pushaway and your first step and to eliminate potential delivery problems if you learn how to recognize errors in coordination between the pushaway and the first step before they cause other problems. Some common errors and suggestions on how to correct them follow.

ERROR   **CORRECTION**

1. You take your first step on the toe or with a shuffle.

1. Step out by lifting the foot off the approach just as you would if you were taking a walk. Think to yourself, "Heel-toe."

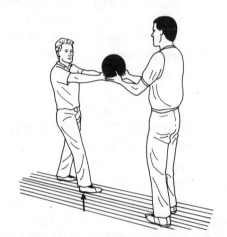

2. You push the ball away too slowly or after you have begun the first step.

2. Push the ball faster, not sooner than your first step. Be sure to start moving the ball and your foot at the same instant, but not at the same speed.

3. You push the ball away too fast or earlier than the first step.

3. Begin pushing the ball as you begin to move your foot. Regulate the speed of the pushaway so that the ball reaches the locked-elbows position as the heel touches down on the count of "one."

4. Your upper body follows the ball forward in the pushaway.

4. Keep the muscles of your spine rigid to counteract the weight of the ball moving forward. Think to yourself, "Walk tall and be snooty."

First Step/Pushaway Coordination Drills

1. No-Ball Coordination

Do not use your ball in this drill. Assume an otherwise normal setup position. Work with a partner face-to-face.

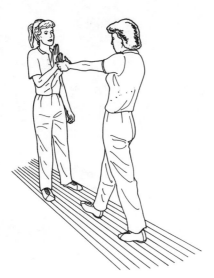

Stand as if you were holding a ball; run through your usual series of setup checks. Your partner should hold one palm up, like a traffic officer signaling a stop, 2 to 3 inches higher than your hands in your setup position. Your partner's hand represents your pushaway destination.

To sharpen your concept of timing, be sure to count your subdivided cadence as in Step 3, Drill 1:

"AND one AND two AND three AND four AND one AND two AND three AND four AND," and so on.

On the "AND" after "four," begin your push and your step; push your bowling arm out crisply with your balance hand. Step out slowly with your swingside foot. Do not move your balance-side, or sliding, foot.

On "one," the back of your bowling fingers touch your partner's palm and your *heel* touches down on the approach. Lock both elbows at the extended position.

Concentrate on the imaginary click of locking your elbows, the real tap of your swingside heel, and the pat of your fingers on your partner's palm—all occurring at the same instant (perfect timing).

Success Goal = 25 consecutive well-timed repetitions

Your Score = (#) _____ repetitions

2. Ball Coordination

Use your ball in this drill. Your partner stands face-to-face with you and is ready to accept your ball when it is in your extended pushaway position. Assume a normal setup and begin by counting your cadence as in the previous drill.

On the "AND" after "four," begin your push and your step; push your bowling arm out crisply with your balance hand. Step out slowly with your swingside foot. Do not move your balance-side foot.

On "one," the ball arrives in your partner's hands and your *heel* touches down on the approach. Lock both elbows at the extended position.

Concentrate on the imaginary click of your elbows, the real tap of your swingside heel, and the arrival of your ball in your partner's hands occurring at the same instant.

Success Goal = 25 consecutive well-timed step and pushaway combinations

Your Score = (#) _____ repetitions

3. Late Ball Timing Awareness

The objective of this drill is to demonstrate the feel of a late pushaway. You will deliberately delay your pushaway so you can study the feel. Use your ball in this drill, setting up and counting as in the two previous drills.

On the "AND" after "four," step out with your swingside foot, but wait until the count of "one" to begin your pushaway.

On "one," your *heel* touches down on the approach, but your ball arrives in your partner's hands later. Be sure to lock both elbows at the extended position.

Concentrate on the awkward feel of the late pushaway. You may feel yourself pushing the ball away faster to catch up with your step.

Success Goal = alternate 5 late pushaways with 5 correctly timed pushaways

Your Score = (#) _____ total pushaways

4. Early Ball Timing Awareness

The objective of this drill is to demonstrate the feel of an early pushaway. You will deliberately force a premature pushaway (before you start your first step) so you can study the feel. Use your ball in this drill, setting up and counting as in the three previous drills.

On the "AND" after "four," begin your pushaway, but wait until the count of "one" to step out with your swingside foot.

On "one," your ball arrives in your partner's hands, but your heel touches down on the approach later.

Concentrate on the awkward feel of early pushaway. You may feel yourself being pulled by the ball toward your partner because your center of gravity has moved to a point in front of your body. Your body feels that it must move forward faster to regain balance.

Success Goal = alternate 5 early pushaways with 5 correctly timed pushaways

Your Score = (#) _____ total pushaways

5. 300 Drill

This drill involves scoring a game without actually counting the pins knocked down. Ask your partner to evaluate your ability to incorporate your first step with your pushaway into your delivery.

Be sure to use proper strike-targeting techniques on every ball. Don't worry about picking up spares, just concentrate on using the skills you've learned so far.

If you execute correctly on your first ball, mark a strike on your scoresheet. If you do not execute correctly on your first ball, mark 6 points. If you execute correctly on your second ball, mark a spare. If you do not execute correctly on your second ball, mark a miss. Tally your points to get as close as possible to a perfect "300" game.

Success Goal = 225 out of 300 possible points

Your Score = (#) _____ points

Step 11 Refine Four Skills

By combining your coordinated upper-body movements (pushaway, pendulum swing, and takeaway) with your lower-body movements (footwork), you are actually performing a coordinated trial delivery.

As before, you will fit your footwork to your swing, and all your movements to your cadence.

Again, your goal for this step is not to get a strike or to hit any particular pin. Your goal is proper execution only. Do not be concerned with pinfall.

WHY IS THE COORDINATED TRIAL DELIVERY IMPORTANT?

The trial delivery represents an opportunity to coordinate learned upper-body movements with learned lower-body movements. You will refine your delivery to eliminate any problems you might be having.

Coordinated Trial Delivery Drills

1. Unassisted Trial Delivery

Assume a normal setup at the appropriate location at the back of the approach. Begin your cadence. Use a heel-toe walking pattern; remember not to place one foot in front of the other as in walking a straight line, not to step side-to-side, and not to cross one foot in front of the other.

First Step: On the "AND" after "four," push your ball with your balance hand and step out with your swingside foot so that your elbows lock and your swingside heel makes contact on the count of "one." Take normal, heel-toe walking steps; concentrate on the feel of your weight being transferred from the heel, through the arch, and to the toe as you walk forward.

Second Step: Begin your second heel-toe step by lifting your sliding foot on the "AND" after "one" so that its heel touches back down on "two." Do not bend your knees or hesitate on any count. Your ball should be at its lowest point in the downswing.

Third Step: Begin your third heel-toe step on the "AND" after "two" by stepping forward with your swingside foot. On "three" its heel should touch down, preparing this foot for pushing the sliding foot. Do not bend your knees yet. Your ball should be at the top of the backswing, neither moving up nor coming down.

Fourth Step: Begin your fourth step on the "AND" after "three," by lifting your sliding foot off the approach and beginning to bend your swingside knee. Your sliding foot's sole should touch down on the approach at the beginning of the slide. Push forward, lowering your hips. Keep your back upright and your shoulders stable as your ball moves in the forward swing, from the top of the backswing to the release point.

Release: Keep your wrist firm. Your thumb should exit the ball just before the ball passes your center of gravity (at the bottom of the forward swing), and your fingers should continue to lift the ball onto the lane surface (to project it) and exit after the ball passes your center of gravity. Keep your swingside sole planted firmly where it was when you began your slide, keep your hips and shoulders perpendicular to your swing, and keep your back straight, almost perpendicular to the approach.

Follow-Through: *Pose* at the foul line until the ball is at least halfway down the lane; try to maintain the balance of the sitting-tall position that your well-timed delivery has given you.

Make all your movements flow together into one graceful sequence. Especially concentrate on the feel of being in time during the delivery and on the feeling of good leverage during your push toward the foul line.

Practice this drill until you feel that you can repeat it easily. Then perform 2 well-executed repetitions for each characteristic listed in the chart below. Give yourself one point for each time you can recall having felt each characteristic.

Success Goal = 15 out of 20 possible points

Characteristic	Trial number	
	1	2
Counted cadence	_____	_____
Pushaway and step in time	_____	_____
Back held upright	_____	_____
Heel-toe steps	_____	_____
Swingside knee bend	_____	_____
Push to foul line	_____	_____
Firm wrist at release	_____	_____
Good finger leverage	_____	_____
Pose at the foul line	_____	_____
Good balance	_____	_____

Your Score = (#) _____ total points

2. 300 Drill

This drill involves scoring a game without actually counting the pins knocked down. Ask your partner to evaluate your ability to coordinate your upper-body movements (pushaway, pendulum swing, and takeaway) with your lower-body movements (footwork).

Be sure to use proper strike-targeting techniques on every ball. Don't worry about picking up spares, just concentrate on using the skills you've learned so far.

If you execute correctly on your first ball, mark a strike on your scoresheet. If you do not execute correctly on your first ball, mark 5 points. If you execute correctly on your second ball, mark a spare. If you do not execute correctly on your second ball, mark a miss. Tally your points to get as close as possible to a perfect ''300' game.

Success Goal = 225 out of 300 possible points

Your Score = (#) _____ points

Step 12   **Finish**

In your delivery, the finish is the coordinated movement of your upper and lower body that begins with your swingside foot's touching down (in preparation for the slide) and ends with the completed follow-through. The objective is to get the ball and the sliding foot moving together toward the foul line.

The well-executed finish is not difficult to refine. It is only a *one-step delivery* made up of three elements that you already know: the setup; the coordinated pushaway, pendulum swing, and takeaway; and the "Power Push."

WHY IS THE FINISH IMPORTANT?

The high-quality finish allows consistently accurate projection of your ball onto the lane with more power. This is due to your using the larger and stronger muscles of your back and legs to do the job while you hold your shoulders perpendicular to your swing plane. A high-quality finish is the result of a superior setup, a well-coordinated pushaway, a graceful pendulum swing, and a well-timed foot-work pattern. In essence, every thing you do in your four-step delivery—from your setup through your first three steps—prepares you for a strong, well-balanced finish.

The ideal finishing body orientation is sitting tall, a position of potential power. In order to effectively use this power, your body must be stabilized so that it can effectively support the forward swing and release. For stability, your feet must be apart, your shoulders and hips perpendicular to your swing, and your back straight as you are releasing the ball.

Because all of the forces generated during your approach reach their peak during your slide and release, the finish puts a great amount of stress on your joints and muscles. You should practice the finish often for two main reasons. First, you must constantly refresh your mind with the feel of a proper finish so that you can analyze and trouble-shoot any delivery. Second, you need to strengthen and maintain the back and leg muscles involved in the finish in order to accommodate the additional stresses.

Detecting Finish Errors

The finish should be taken unhurried, with the speed of the slide matching the speed of the ball in the forward swing. Your back should be upright as it was in the setup.

You can increase the consistency with which you execute a high-quality finish if you learn to recognize common errors.

ERROR ⊘	CORRECTION
1. You step, not slide, forward to the foul line.	1. When your ball reaches the top of the backswing, slide forward; do not lift your sliding foot off the approach.
2. You lean over.	2. Keep your back upright.
3. You drop your bowling shoulder.	3. Keep your shoulders level; stretch your balance arm out, down, and back.
4. You "double bounce" the ball (hit the approach with the ball before you have released it).	4. Do not lean over; keep your shoulders straight and take it easy. Lower your hips gently; do not lunge.
5. You loft the ball (hold on too long and toss it too far out into the lane).	5. Simply let your ball swing down on its own. Keep your wrist firm; do not squeeze the grip.
6. You lose balance and step over to your swingside after the release.	6. Bend your swingside leg more deeply as you slide forward.

Finish Drills

1. Power Push Delivery

Assume your normal setup position but, for now, stand approximately 4 feet from the foul line, facing the second arrow. Begin your cadence and focus on your visual target. You will take only a one-step delivery from this position, finishing in a well-balanced, sitting-tall follow-through.

From a standing position, execute a normal pushaway and let the ball fall into its free-pendulum swing. On the "AND" after "three," begin lifting your sliding foot off the approach and bending your swingside knee. On the count of "four," say "push" to yourself and make your sliding sole contact the approach in its step forward; your swingside knee should still be bending. Using your swingside sole as an anchor, push your sliding foot forward toward the foul line.

On the "AND" after "four," say to yourself, "Slide." Keeping your upper body almost perpendicular to the approach (not bent over more than 20 degrees), allow your center of gravity (roughly your hips) to move down toward the approach. Release your ball on the upswing, keeping the same speed as the forward swing.

Note. You may have difficulty maintaining traction with your swingside foot if the shoe's sole is not made of rubber or if it has a leather tip. If this is the case, have a professional shoe repairman cover the entire sole with nonmarring rubber. Do not use plastic or crepe.

In your final resting, or recovery, position, assume and hold the sitting-tall position, with the entire sole and heel of your sliding shoe and the front half of the sole of your swingside shoe still in contact with the approach. You should hold your back as straight, or upright, as it was in your initial setup position.

Practice this drill as many times as necessary to attain the feel of the characteristics of a solid finish. Then perform two well-executed deliveries for each characteristic listed in the following chart. Concentrate on feeling each characteristic. Ask your partner to watch you, giving you one point for each time you successfully perform a characteristic. Compare your recall of a characteristic with your partner's assessment.

Success Goal = 15 out of 20 total points

Characteristic	Trial number	
	1	2
Keeps back straight	_____	_____
Pushaway straight out	_____	_____
Takeaway and downswing in time	_____	_____
Balance arm out	_____	_____
Begins push on ''three''	_____	_____
Begins slide on ''four''	_____	_____
Ball and slide in time	_____	_____
Projects ball onto lane	_____	_____
Sits tall	_____	_____
High follow-through	_____	_____

Your Score = (#) _____ points

2. 300 Drill

This drill involves scoring a game without actually counting the pins knocked down. Ask your partner to evaluate your ability to incorporate a high-quality finish into your delivery.

Be sure to use proper strike-targeting techniques on every ball. Don't worry about picking up spares, just concentrate on using the skills you've learned so far.

If you execute correctly on your first ball, mark a strike on your scoresheet. If you do not execute correctly on your first ball, mark 4 points. If you execute correctly on your second ball, mark a spare. If you do not execute correctly on your second ball, mark a miss. Tally your points to get as close as possible to a perfect ''300'' game.

Success Goal = 225 out of 300 points

Your Score = (#) _____ points

Step 13 Refine Five Skills

With the extensive experience you have gained from the drills in the previous steps, you should have no trouble in performing a smooth, flowing, coordinated finished delivery. Remember to continue fitting your movements to your familiar cadence.

WHY IS THE COORDINATED FINISHED DELIVERY IMPORTANT?

Your finished delivery represents your best technique, the most important thing you do in bowling. Your coordinated finished delivery is the most efficient delivery you can execute. It contains no wasted movements and is not tiring, even when you bowl several games in a row. It also allows for fewer opportunities to commit errors throughout the delivery.

HOW TO EXECUTE THE COORDINATED FINISHED DELIVERY

No instructor or coach expects a performer to remember all cues at all times; paralysis by analysis can become a problem. To help you make your movements more automatic and flowing, you should learn a shortened sequence of cues leading to your finished delivery. This simplification (see Figure 13.1) gives you a clearer concept of your movement and prepares you for structuring your mental practice.

Figure 13.1 Keys to Success: Simplified Cues for the Coordinated Finished Delivery

Preparation Phase

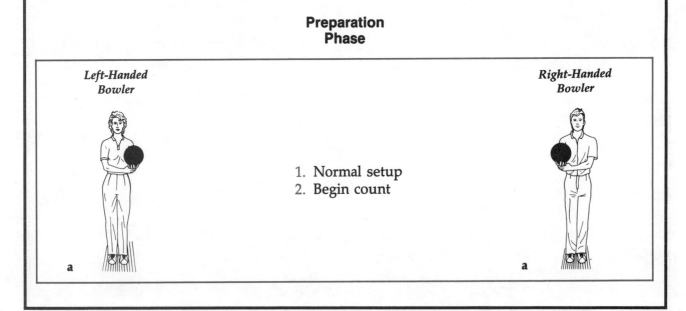

Left-Handed Bowler

Right-Handed Bowler

1. Normal setup
2. Begin count

a

a

Execution Phase

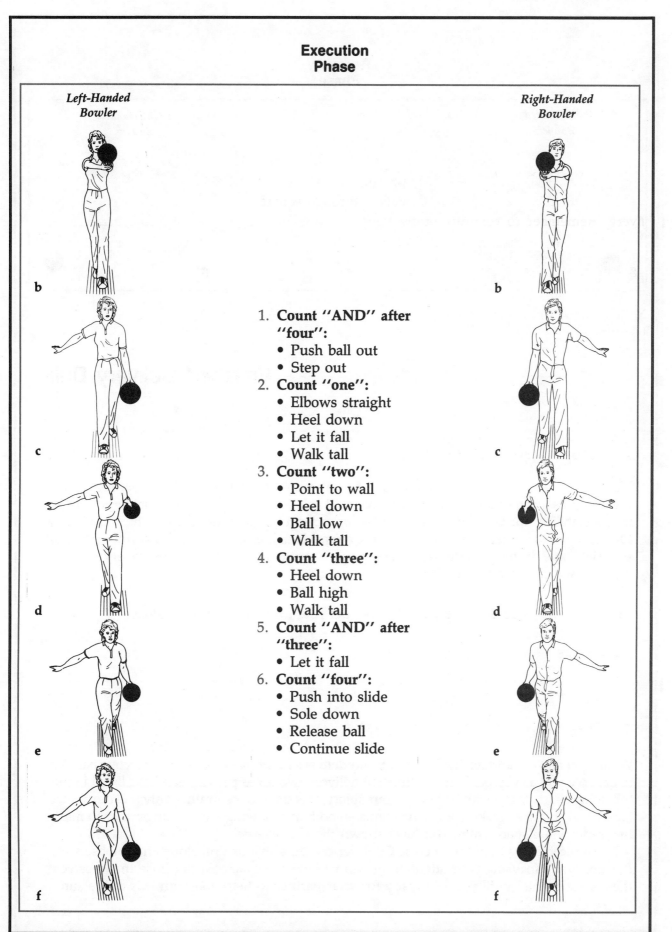

Left-Handed Bowler

Right-Handed Bowler

1. **Count "AND" after "four":**
   - Push ball out
   - Step out
2. **Count "one":**
   - Elbows straight
   - Heel down
   - Let it fall
   - Walk tall
3. **Count "two":**
   - Point to wall
   - Heel down
   - Ball low
   - Walk tall
4. **Count "three":**
   - Heel down
   - Ball high
   - Walk tall
5. **Count "AND" after "three":**
   - Let it fall
6. **Count "four":**
   - Push into slide
   - Sole down
   - Release ball
   - Continue slide

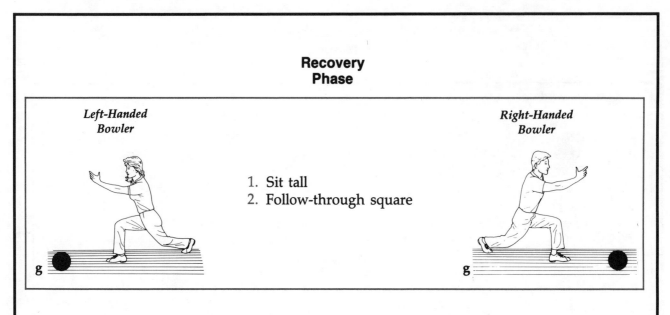

Recovery Phase

Left-Handed Bowler

Right-Handed Bowler

1. Sit tall
2. Follow-through square

Finished Delivery Drills

1. Simplified Cue Delivery

Now use the Keys to Success (Figure 13.1) for 18 setups and deliveries. For every setup, use the two cues listed under "Preparation Phase." Lock in strongly on your visual target, using it as a stabilizer for your head and count your cadence for consistency. For the "Execution Phase," take three deliveries for each of the counts listed, grouping cues by count at the appropriate time during your delivery. Make your movements flow. For the "Recovery Phase," use the two cues for each delivery.

Success Goal = 18 deliveries, 3 deliveries per count under "Execution Phase"

Your Score = (#) _____ total deliveries

2. How Good Is Your Form?

When you feel comfortable with the finished delivery in the previous drill, ask your partner to observe you as you perform the finished delivery two times per characteristic listed in the following chart. Execute to the best of your ability, this time concentrating only on your visual target and trying to make your movements smooth and flowing. Ask your partner to mark the appropriate space when you have shown the characteristic.

If you receive less than the Success Goal, repeat the previous drill alone and unobserved. Practice while focusing your attention on your weakest characteristics (those that received the fewest points) until you feel ready for your partner to help you with this drill again.

Success Goal = 25 out of 30 possible points

Characteristic	Trial number	
	1	2
Back straight	_____	_____
Pushaway straight out	_____	_____
Pushaway not rounded	_____	_____
Pushaway in time	_____	_____
Takeaway and downswing in time	_____	_____
Balance arm out	_____	_____
Heel–toe steps	_____	_____
Knees not bent	_____	_____
Ball and slide in time	_____	_____
Push into slide	_____	_____
Projection of ball	_____	_____
Sitting tall	_____	_____
High follow-through	_____	_____
Rhythm consistent	_____	_____
Movement flows	_____	_____

Your Score = (#) _____ points

3. Bowl for Score

This drill involves scoring a game using your coordinated finished delivery. Use regulation scoring. To pick up spares at this point, experiment with walking in the direction of the pins.

Success Goal = bowl a complete game

Your Score = _____

Coordinated Finished Delivery Keys to Success Checklist

Remember that the coordinated finished delivery you have learned is easier to troubleshoot when you bowl frequently, and to "whip" back into shape after a layoff. Because you now know how the various elements of the properly executed delivery are supposed to feel, you possess internal standards with which to compare any performance. Thus, you can keep yourself under control, performing more consistently over a longer period of time, and bowling will become an enjoyable lifetime activity! As necessary, ask your teacher, coach, or trained observer to qualitatively evaluate your technique according to the following checklist.

Preparation Phase

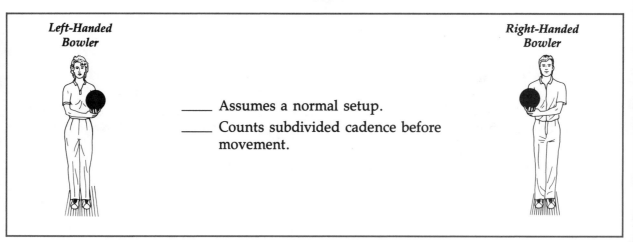

Left-Handed Bowler

Right-Handed Bowler

____ Assumes a normal setup.
____ Counts subdivided cadence before movement.

Execution
Phase

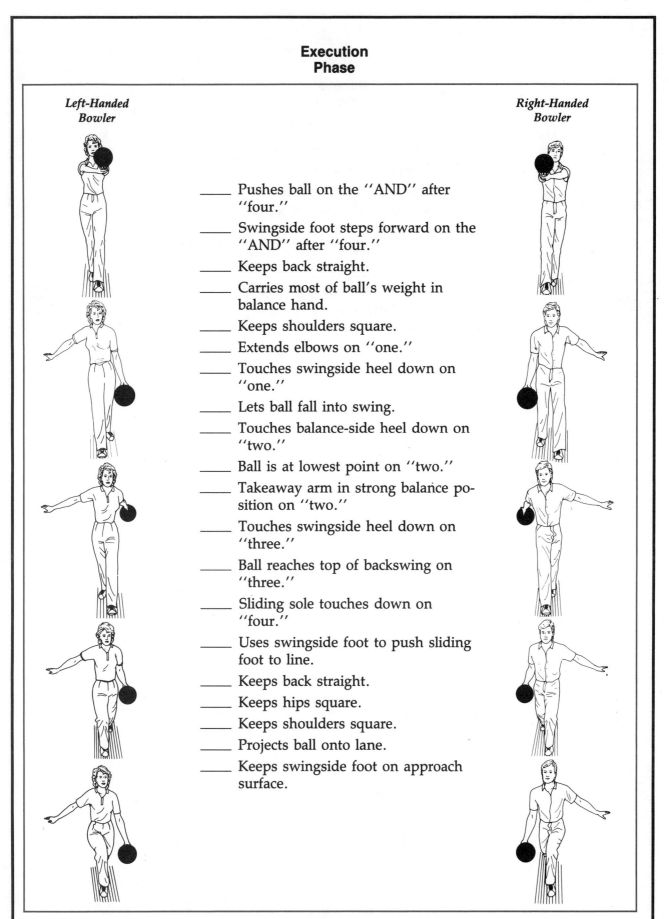

**Left-Handed
Bowler**

**Right-Handed
Bowler**

_____ Pushes ball on the "AND" after "four."

_____ Swingside foot steps forward on the "AND" after "four."

_____ Keeps back straight.

_____ Carries most of ball's weight in balance hand.

_____ Keeps shoulders square.

_____ Extends elbows on "one."

_____ Touches swingside heel down on "one."

_____ Lets ball fall into swing.

_____ Touches balance-side heel down on "two."

_____ Ball is at lowest point on "two."

_____ Takeaway arm in strong balance position on "two."

_____ Touches swingside heel down on "three."

_____ Ball reaches top of backswing on "three."

_____ Sliding sole touches down on "four."

_____ Uses swingside foot to push sliding foot to line.

_____ Keeps back straight.

_____ Keeps hips square.

_____ Keeps shoulders square.

_____ Projects ball onto lane.

_____ Keeps swingside foot on approach surface.

Recovery
Phase

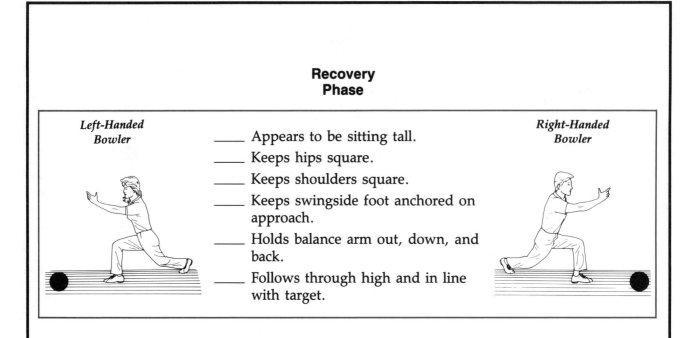

Left-Handed Bowler

_____ Appears to be sitting tall.

_____ Keeps hips square.

_____ Keeps shoulders square.

_____ Keeps swingside foot anchored on approach.

_____ Holds balance arm out, down, and back.

_____ Follows through high and in line with target.

Right-Handed Bowler

Step 14 Spare Targeting

You have been consistently rolling your straight ball or hook ball over a target line. Now, you apply that skill to the second ball of a frame to try to knock down all the pins left standing after your strike-ball attempt to make a spare. *Spare targeting* is basically identical to strike targeting, with one important exception: the desired pin impact point changes with each spare leave.

WHY IS SPARE TARGETING IMPORTANT?

In order to be a well-rounded bowler, you should be able to *pick up* (*cover*, or *convert*) any reasonable spare leave you may encounter. You must put as much thought and effort into picking up spares as you put into making strikes. Regardless of the type of competition, if you patiently and persistently convert your spares, you can avoid really low games and stay in the running until you begin to strike more frequently. Remember, you can average 190 even if you never get a strike. Spare leaves provide an element of variety, and you should think of them as opportunities to become more accurate and more versatile. If you set your mind this way and are willing to remember some simple rules and numbers, you will become a superior spare bowler.

HOW TO EXECUTE SPARE TARGETING

There are approximately 250 spare leaves that you will commonly encounter, but this number becomes manageable when you realize that there are only a few angles from which all of them may be converted. Once you have properly aligned your straight or hook ball for a strike, the adjustments you must make for spare targeting are of the same proportion and direction. In other words, it matters little

whether you roll a straight ball or a hook ball—the adjustments for spares are similar.

You can make some spares, called *pocket spares*, by shooting your strike target line, in which case no adjustment is necessary. Other leaves may best be converted by moving your feet to another setup location; still others may best be made by moving your target point (and, thus, your visual target) and your feet.

In this step, you will again use the second arrow as your strike target. However, when you bowl on your own in a game situation, you may have to use a totally different strike target point—for example, the first arrow, the third arrow, a board between arrows, or even one of the small dots between the foul line and the arrows. Regardless of what your target point is, you will be using some target line for your strike ball.

Before attempting any spare shots, you must first be aligned properly for your strike ball. Your points of reference for all spare attempts are your strike target and the setup location appropriate for this strike target. Although you may have to make minor adjustments to some of the setup locations prescribed in the following drills, the principles you now learn will still apply to all game situations.

SPARE PRINCIPLES

Learn the following principles thoroughly. They will make you a better spare bowler by allowing you to play spares through intelligent planning, increasing the probability of your spare conversion before you even roll your ball. While reading these principles, look at a diagram, a picture, or an actual full rack of pins and try to identify the pins being discussed.

1. If your spare leave is to the inside, move your setup location to the outside; if the leave is outside, move your setup to the inside (see Figure 14.1).

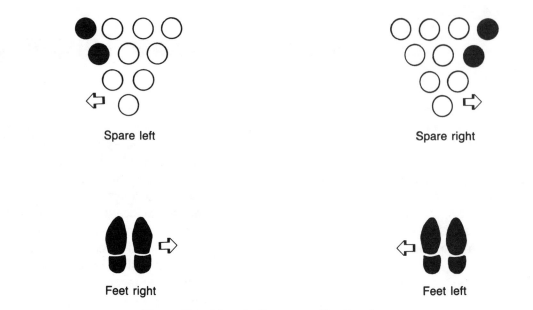

Figure 14.1 Move in the proper direction for spares.

2. Always walk toward your spare leave; walk parallel with your spare target line (see Figure 14.2).

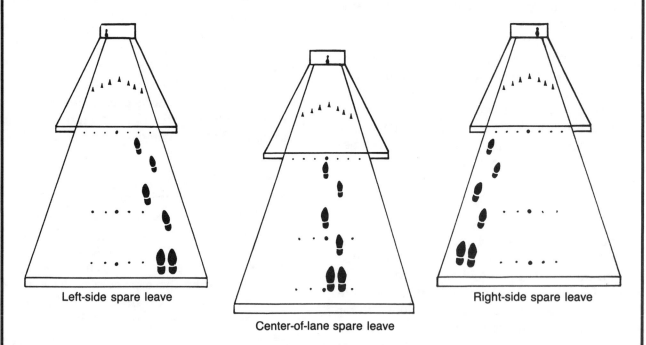

Figure 14.2 Walk toward your spare leave.

3. Always choose a spare impact point that allows your ball to hit the pin closest to you first (see Figure 14.3).

Figure 14.3 Spare impact point: (a) incorrect placement, (b) correct placement.

4. Always choose a spare impact point that allows your ball to contact the most pins. This minimizes the chance of hitting only the front pins while missing the ones farther back, an act called *chopping*. Unless you are attempting to convert a *split*, a leave in which more than one pin is missing between two standing pins, do not depend on your ball to *carom*, or bounce, pins into other pins to make spares (see Figure 14.4).

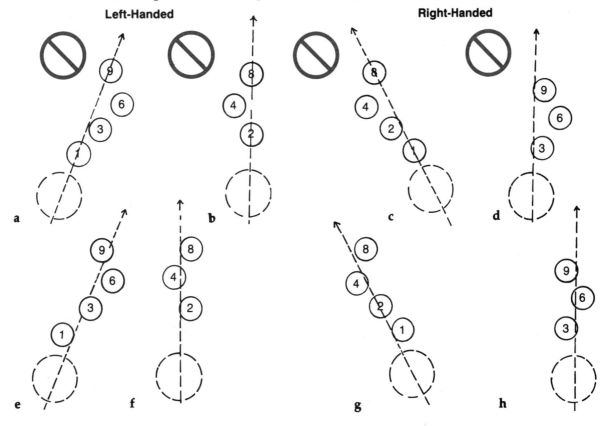

Figure 14.4 Spare impact points: ball should contact the most pins in a spare leave; incorrect impact point shown in a-d; correct impact point shown in e-h.

5. Always first *translate* your spare leave into a simpler one before deciding on how to shoot it. The pin leave to which it is translated may not even be part of the actual leave; the translation can be a *psychologically* less difficult leave. For example, the 3-10 split can be translated as the much easier 6-pin shot because the ball will contact both the 3 pin and the 10 pin by rolling down the board upon which the 6 pin usually rests. Likewise, the 5-10 split translates as a 2-pin shot, the 2-4-5-8 as an 8-pin shot, the 4-10 split as a 7-pin shot, and so on (see Figure 14.5).

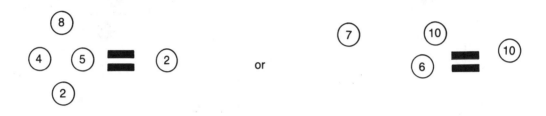

Figure 14.5 Translate the spare into an easier one.

6. After you have translated your spare leave, fit to it one of the seven spare target lines detailed later, in the drills, then make appropriate adjustments of your target line and setup location from your original strike target line (see Figure 14.6).

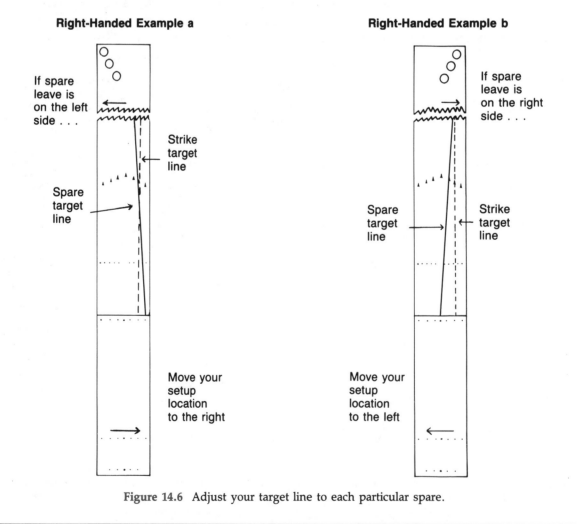

Figure 14.6 Adjust your target line to each particular spare.

Effective spare targeting using the target line system is nothing more than becoming skilled at carrying out the mental checklist illustrated in Figure 14.7.

Figure 14.7   Keys to Success: Spare Targeting

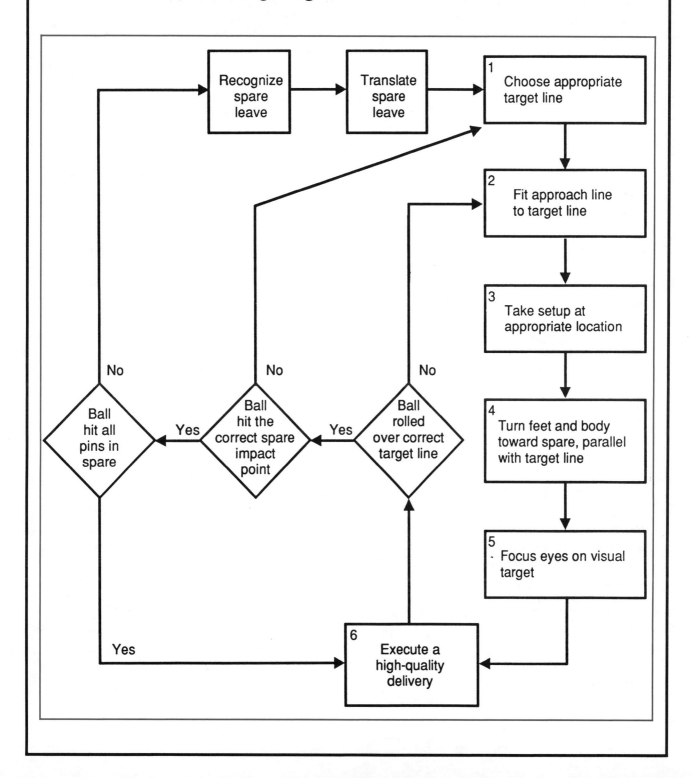

DETECTING SPARE-TARGETING ERRORS

Common errors in spare targeting have been considered in the previous principles. If you strictly adhere to these principles before stepping up onto the approach to attempt a spare, you will significantly minimize spare-targeting errors. If you do not, you may attempt a spare using a poorly selected target line, thereby missing the spare before you ever roll the ball.

Any errors that occur after you have chosen the correct spare impact point and a correct target line would involve general problems in hitting any target line. For these, refer to the "Detecting Errors" sections of Step 6 for applicable information; simply substitute the words *spare* for *strike* and *spare impact point* for *pocket* or *strike pocket* in those examples.

For more information on spare targeting, see Ritger and Allen (1978).

Spare-Targeting Drills

Note on the Headings:

Category is a way of classifying the type of spare; it does not refer to the spare impact point or to the translation.

Common examples are a few of the spares you will frequently encounter. Because comparable spare leaves are numbered differently for right- and left-handed (RH; LH) bowlers, it is necessary to customize the following drills. A statement without a reference to handedness, though, applies to all bowlers.

Spare impact point is the approximate place, or board number, where your spare ball should contact the translated spare leave.

Change in visual target indicates the number of boards something is different from the strike target line positions. "+" means "boards added (toward the inside)," and "−" means "boards subtracted (toward the outside)." For example, a "+8" move of your feet (your setup location) means that you would move your feet 8 boards farther from your swingside channel than your strike setup location. A "−5" move means that you would move 5 boards closer to the swingside channel than your strike setup location.

Change in setup location indicates that you should make the appropriate adjustments to your target line and setup location. Before attempting any of the following drills, take a warm-up to find your strike target line, using the second arrow as your target point and visual target. Concentrate on keeping your body square to your target line (shoulders and hips parallel with each other and 90 degrees to the target line)—not necessarily to the foul line—as you move your target line diagonally across the lane.

You may discover that the prescribed setup location for a given spare target line must be adjusted to suit your unique delivery. In order for you to be more accurate, you are encouraged to make adjustments in 1-board increments to the inside or to the outside of the suggested setup location. Record it as the "most accurate setup location" at the end of each drill. You will use this information to complete the "Corrected Setup Location Chart" at the end of Drill 7. Roll all spare drill balls at a full rack of pins, directing your ball toward the assigned pin in each of the following drills.

1. Pocket Spares

Left-Handed Bowler

Category 1-pin and 5-pin single and combination leaves

Common examples 1, 5, 1-2, 1-5, 1-10, 1-8, 1-3-5, 1-3-8, 1-2-5, 1-2-4, 1-2-8, 1-2-4-7, 2-5, 5-8, 5-9

Right-Handed Bowler

Category 1-pin and 5-pin single and combination leaves

Common examples 1, 5, 1-3, 1-5, 1-7, 1-9, 1-2-5, 1-2-9, 1-3-5, 1-3-6, 1-3-9, 1-3-6-10, 3-5, 5-8, 5-9

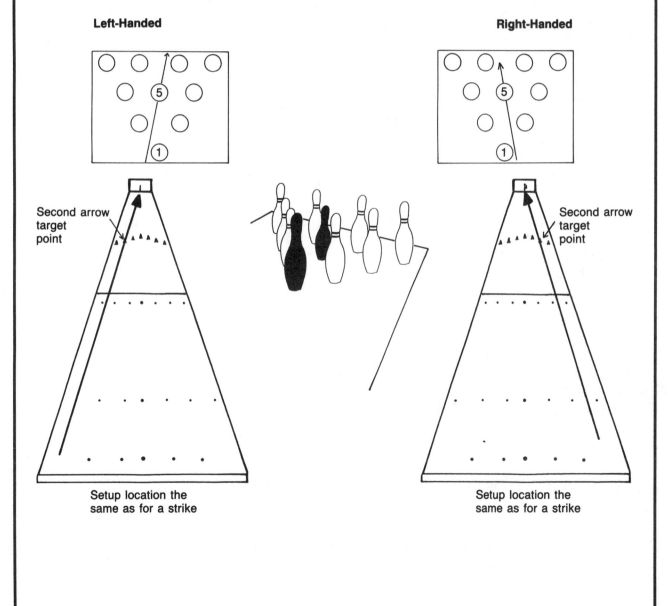

Left-Handed

Right-Handed

Second arrow target point

Second arrow target point

Setup location the same as for a strike

Setup location the same as for a strike

All Bowlers

Spare impact point The strike pocket

Change in visual target None (still the second arrow)

Change in setup location None

Prepare a scoresheet, using the Sample Scoresheet as a model. A blank scoresheet is available in Appendix B.

Sample Scoresheet

Write:
"+" if you hit the pocket (board #17)

Desired pin
impact board number
"-" if you did not

NAME	1	2	3	4	5	6	7	8	9	10
Jane	17 − / 18	17 − / 19	17 − / 20	17 + / 21	17 + / 21	17 + / 21				

Setup location

Three plus entries in a row
allow you to go to next drill

Deliver your ball at a full rack of pins, disregarding pin reaction. If you hit the pocket squarely, put a "+" in the small box in the upper right corner of the appropriate frame of your scoresheet; if not, enter a "−" sign. Do not, however, record any entry unless you executed your shot well and hit your spare target line.

Make 1-board adjustments to your setup location if necessary, and record the new setup location in the appropriate frame. In the space marked "Your Score," write the board number of the setup location that allows you the most accuracy.

Repeat this drill until you hit the pocket squarely 3 times in succession with proper execution each time, then proceed to the next drill. Because you will use the same scoresheet and continue from one drill to the other on the same game line, your ideal is to have all "+" entries from the first to the last frames for all of the drills.

Success Goal =

a. identify your most accurate setup location

b. hit the selected spare impact point 3 times in 3 attempts

Your Score =

a. (+ or −) _____ boards from the strike target setup location

b. (#) _____ hits out of (#) _____ attempts

2. *Near-Inside (Balance Side) Spares*

Left-Handed Bowler

Category   3-pin single and combination leaves

Common examples   1, 3, 9, 1-7, 3-5, 3-6, 3-9, 1-3-6, 1-3-7, 1-3-9, 1-3-10, 3-5-6, 1-3-6-7, 1-3-6-10, 3-5-6-9, 5-6

Spare impact point   3 pin

Right-Handed Bowler

Category   2-pin single and combination leaves

Common examples   1, 2, 8, 1-10, 2-4, 2-5, 2-8, 1-2-4, 1-2-7, 1-2-8, 1-2-10, 2-4-5, 1-2-4-7, 1-2-4-10, 2-4-5-8, 4-5

Spare impact point   2 pin

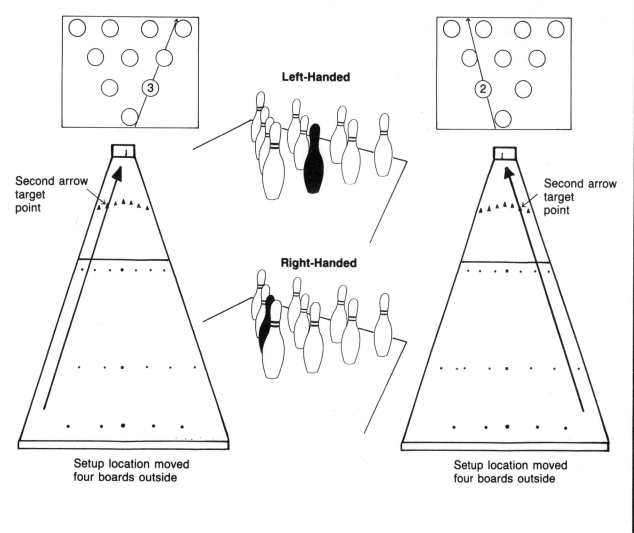

All Bowlers

Change in visual target   None (still second arrow)

Change in setup location   4 boards to the outside (-4)

Continue using the same scoresheet from the previous drill, keeping score in the same way. With the 2 pin (RH) or 3 pin (LH) as your intended impact pin, use the second arrow as your target point on the lane and move your feet to a setup location 4 boards outside your strike location. Record the spare impact point and the board number of your new setup location as before. Deliver your ball properly at the full rack, recording a "+" for a square hit on the impact pin and a "$-$" for any other type of hit.

Make 1-board adjustments to your setup location if necessary, and record the new setup location in the appropriate frame. In the space marked "Your Score," write the board number of the setup location that allows you the most accuracy.

Repeat this drill until you hit the pin squarely 3 times in succession, then proceed to the next drill. Are you on your way to all "+" entries?

Success Goal =

   a. identify your most accurate setup location

   b. hit the selected spare impact point 3 times in 3 attempts

Your Score =

   a. (+ or $-$) _____ boards from the strike target setup location

   b. (#) _____ hits out of (#) _____ attempts

3. Medium-Inside (Balance Side) Spares

Left-Handed Bowler

Category   6-pin single and combination leaves

Common examples   6, 6-9, 6-10, 3-7, 3-10, 3-5-6

Spare impact point   6 pin

Right-Handed Bowler

Category   4-pin single and combination leaves

Common examples   4, 4-7, 4-8, 2-7, 2-10, 2-4-5

Spare impact point   4 pin

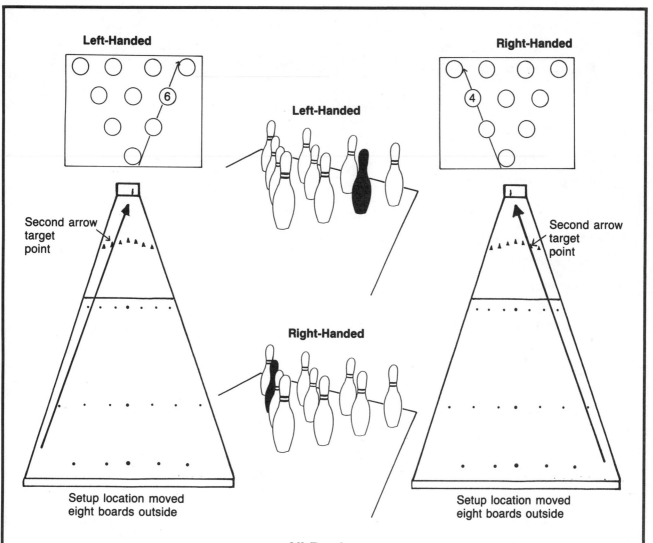

Left-Handed

Right-Handed

Left-Handed

Second arrow
target
point

Setup location moved
eight boards outside

Right-Handed

Second arrow
target
point

Setup location moved
eight boards outside

All Bowlers

Change in visual target None (still the second arrow)

Change in setup location 8 boards to the outside (−8)

With the 4 pin (RH) or 6 pin (LH) as your intended impact pin, use the second arrow as your target point on the lane and move your feet to a setup location 8 boards outside your strike location. Record the spare impact point and the board number of your new setup location. Deliver your ball at a full rack, making entries as before. Make and record adjustments in your setup location as in the previous drills.

Repeat this drill until you hit the pin squarely 3 times in succession, then proceed to the next drill. How long is your string of ''+'' entries?

Success Goal =

a. identify your most accurate setup location

b. hit the selected spare impact point 3 times in 3 attempts

Your Score =

a. (+ or −) _____ boards from the strike target setup location

b. (#) _____ hits out of (#) _____ attempts

4. Far-Inside (Balance Side) Corner Pin Spares

Left-Handed Bowler

Category   10-pin single

Common examples   10, 6-7, 6-8, 6-7-10, 6-8-10

Spare impact point   10 pin

Right-Handed Bowler

Category   7-pin single

Common examples   7, 4-9, 4-10, 4-7-9, 4-7-10

Spare impact point   7 pin

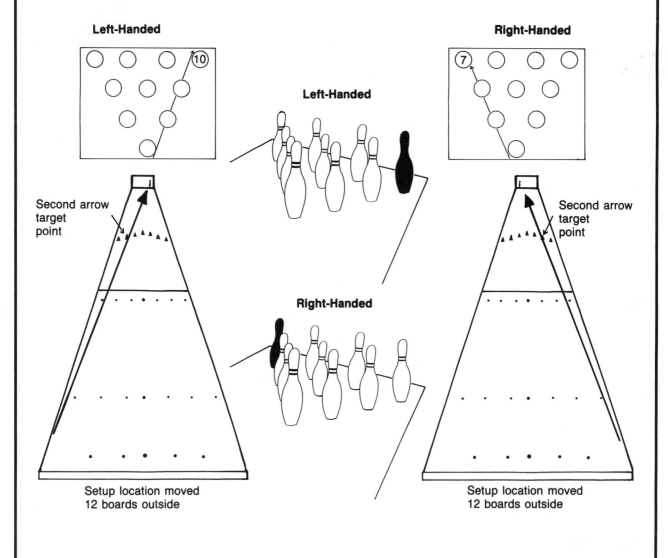

Left-Handed

Left-Handed

Right-Handed

Right-Handed

Second arrow target point

Second arrow target point

Setup location moved 12 boards outside

Setup location moved 12 boards outside

All Bowlers

Change in visual target   None (still second arrow)

Change in setup location   12 boards to the outside (−12)

With the 7 pin (RH) or 10 pin (LH) as your intended impact pin, use the second arrow as your target point on the lane and move your feet to a setup location 12 boards outside your strike location. Record the spare impact point and the board number of your new setup location. Deliver your ball at a full rack, making entries as before. Make and record adjustments in your setup location as before.

Repeat this drill until you hit the pin squarely 3 times in succession, then proceed to the next drill. Are you stringing together ''+'' entries?

Success Goal =

a. identify your most accurate setup location

b. hit the selected spare impact point 3 times in 3 attempts

Your Score =

a. (+ or −) _____ boards from the strike target setup location

b. (#) _____ hits out of (#) _____ attempts

5. Near-Outside (Swingside) Spares

Left-Handed Bowler

Category   2-pin single and combination leaves

Common examples   2, 8, 2-4, 2-5, 2-8, 4-5, 5-10, 2-4-5, 2-4-7, 2-4-8, 2-5-8, 2-4-5-8

Spare impact point   2 pin

Right-Handed Bowler

Category   3-pin single and combination leaves

Common examples   3, 9, 3-5, 3-6, 3-9, 5-6, 5-7, 3-5-6, 3-5-9, 3-6-9, 3-6-10, 3-5-6-9

Spare impact point   3 pin

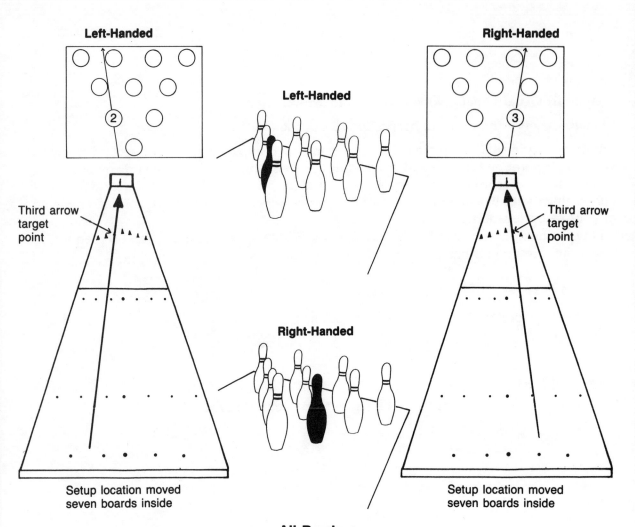

Left-Handed

Right-Handed

Left-Handed

Right-Handed

Third arrow
target
point

Third arrow
target
point

Setup location moved
seven boards inside

Setup location moved
seven boards inside

All Bowlers

Change in visual target   To third arrow (+5)

Change in setup location   7 boards to the inside (+7)

With the 3 pin (RH) or 2 pin (LH) as your intended impact pin, use the third arrow as your target point on the lane and move your feet to a setup location 7 boards inside your strike location. Record the spare impact point and the board number of your new setup location. Deliver your ball at a full rack, making entries as before. Make and record adjustments in your setup location as before.

Repeat this drill until you hit the pin squarely 3 times in succession, then proceed to the next drill. How are the ''+'' entries coming along?

Success Goal =

a. identify your most accurate setup location

b. hit the selected spare impact point 3 times in 3 attempts

Your Score =

a. (+ or −) _____ boards from the strike target setup location

b. (#) _____ hits out of (#) _____ attempts

6. *Medium-Outside (Swingside) Spares*

Left-Handed Bowler

Category   4-pin single and combination leaves

Common examples   4, 2-7, 2-10, 4-7, 4-8, 2-7-10

Spare impact point   4 pin

Right-Handed Bowler

Category   6-pin single and combination leaves

Common examples   6, 3-7, 3-10, 6-9, 6-10, 3-7-10

Spare impact point   6 pin

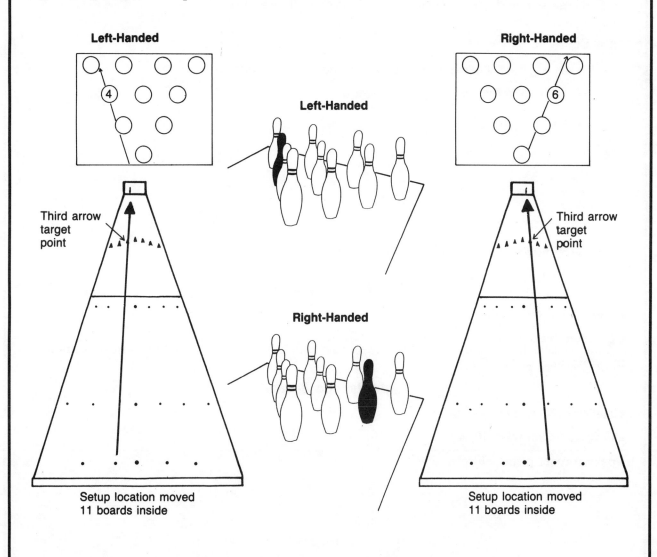

All Bowlers

Change in visual target To third arrow (+5)

Change in setup location 11 boards to the inside (+11)

With the 6 pin (RH) or 4 pin (LH) as your intended impact pin, use the third arrow as your target point on the lane and move your feet to a setup location 11 boards inside your strike location. Record the spare impact point and the board number of your new setup location. Deliver your ball at a full rack, making entries as before. Make and record adjustments to your setup location as before.

Success Goal =

    a. identify your most accurate setup location

    b. hit the selected spare impact point 3 times in 3 attempts

Your Score =

    a. (+ or −) _____ boards from the strike target setup location

    b. (#) _____ hits out of (#) _____ attempts

7. Far-Outside (Swingside) Corner Pin Spares

Left-Handed Bowler

Category 7-pin single

Common examples 7, 4-6, 4-10, 4-7-10, 4-8-10

Spare impact point 7 pin

Right-Handed Bowler

Category 10-pin single

Common examples 10, 4-6, 6-7, 6-7-10, 6-9-10

Spare impact point 10 pin

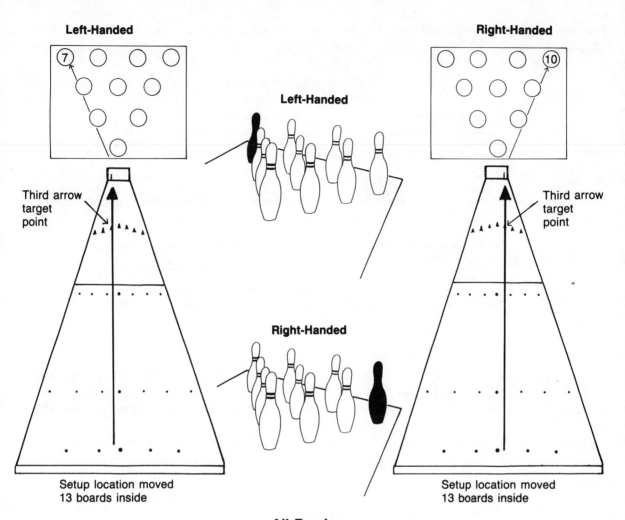

All Bowlers

Change in visual target To third arrow (+5)

Change in setup location 13 boards to the inside (+13)

With the 10 pin (RH) or 7 pin (LH) as your intended impact pin, use the third arrow as your target point on the lane and move your feet to a setup location 13 boards inside your strike location. Record the spare impact point and board number of your new setup location. Roll at a full rack, as in the previous drills. Make and record adjustments in your setup location as before.

Success Goal =

  a. identify your most accurate setup location

  b. hit the selected spare impact point 3 times in 3 attempts

Your Score =

  a. (+ or −) _____ boards from the strike target setup location

  b. (#) _____ hits out of (#) _____ attempts

Stop and complete the ''Corrected Setup Location Chart'' before you move on to the next drill. Transfer into the appropriate boxes all entries made in response to the Success Goal of identifying your most accurate setup location in Drills 1 through 7. Use the new, reliable setup locations on the Corrected Setup Location Chart, attempting different spare target lines in the future.

Corrected Setup Location Chart

Spare category	Most accurate setup location[a]
Pocket spares	No Change
Near inside	
Medium inside	
Far inside corner pin	
Near outside	
Medium outside	
Far outside corner pin	

[a]Expressed by number of boards inside (+) or outside (-) the strike setup location.

8. Spare Cleanup

Bowl three games with a partner. In the first frame of the first game, your partner will roll the first ball practicing good strike targeting technique. You will attempt to pick up any remaining pins. In the second frame, you roll the first ball and let your partner convert the spare. Continue alternating throughout the three games.

After each game, divide the number of successful spare conversions by the number of times you attempted to make a spare. Multiply this number by 100 to obtain a percentage score that will help you track your success.

Success Goal = 80% spare conversion in any one game

Game number

	1	2	3
Your Score = (%) conversion	_____	_____	_____

9. Corner Pin Sharpshooter

This game involves a high degree of spare-shooting accuracy and some competition. You can play this game in competition against one opponent, or you can team up with a partner and bowl against two opponents, adding your two games to get one doubles-team score. Many variations are possible; you may make up some of your own. Keep your score on a regular scoresheet, but write only points (as follows)—not strikes, spares, or regular pinfall—in the frames.

Point values:

- 7 pin and 10 pin = 10 points each pin
- 4-7-8 and 6-9-10 = 5 points for all three pins
- Knocking down any other pin = 0 points for the frame (includes striking on the first or second ball)
- Ball rolled into channel = minus (−) 20 points

The objective of each frame is to roll a first ball and a second ball, knocking down only the 7 pin and the 10 pin with two shots; this will give you a score of 20 in the frame. Less accuracy may result in your knocking down the 4-7-8 and 6-9-10 combinations, yielding a total score of 10 in the frame. Knocking down the 10 pin and then the 4-6-8 would give you 15 points in the frame; however, knocking down the 10 pin and then knocking down the 6-9 would reduce the score from 10 to 5 (5 being the value of knocking down the 6-9-10 together). Rolling a ball into the channel on the first attempt (−20) and then hitting only the 7 pin on the second ball (+10) would give a −10 (−20 + 10) for the frame. Only 2 balls are allowed in the tenth frame (see the Scored Frames Example).

Scored Frames Example

Bill / Carla	10 | 10 20	5 | 0 25	10 | 10 45	10 | -20 35	5 | 5 45	-20 | 5 30	10 | 10 50	10 | 5 65	10 | 5 80	5 | 5 90
Holly / Kim	-20 | 10 -10	10 | 5 5	10 | 5 20	10 | 10 40	0 | 5 45	5 | 5 55	5 | 0 60	10 | 10 80	-20 | 10 70	10 | 5 85

Success Goal = outscore your opponent with as high a score as you can bowl (200 points maximum)

		Game number			
		1	2	3	4
Your Score (points) =		_____	_____	_____	_____
Opponent's Score (points) =		_____	_____	_____	_____

10. Call Shot Game

This game involves a higher degree of shooting accuracy and some keen competition.
Point values:

- Make your call (leave standing the exact number of pins declared): you are awarded 10 points
- Do not make your call (leave standing any number of pins other than that declared): your opponent is awarded 10 points
- Make a declared strike: you are awarded 30 points
- Make a strike when not declared: your opponent is awarded 20 points
- Roll a ball into the channel at any time: your opponent is awarded 5 points
- Any spare: 5 points

Game Objective: Before you roll your first ball, you must call, or declare, how many pins you will leave standing. If you leave the *exact number of pins* you called standing, you are awarded the appropriate number of points, and your opponent must try for the extra spare points. If you miss your call, your opponent receives the points and must try for the spare points. If your opponent converts your spare, 5 points are given to your opponent; if not, you receive the 5 points.

Your opponent will roll the first ball of the next frame, and you will alternate roles each frame. Keep track of yours and your opponent's points on separate game lines of a scoresheet; score points—not strikes or spares—in the frames (see Example Call Shot Gamelines).

Example Call Shot Gamelines

NAME	1	2	3	4	5	6	7	8	9	10
1 CARL'S CALLS	X	⊘		⊘		⊘		⊘		⊘
2 CARL'S SCORE	9	5								
	5									
3 SANDY'S CALLS	⊘	X	⊘		⊘		⊘		⊘	
4 SANDY'S SCORE	10	X								
		40								

Play-by-Play: In the first frame, Carl calls a strike but knocks down only 9, giving Sandy 10 points plus a chance to make Carl's spare. She misses, giving Carl 5 points in the first frame and herself 10 points in the first frame.

In the second frame, Sandy calls a strike and knocks down all 10 pins, giving her 30 points, which she adds to the 10 points of the first frame for a total of 40 points in the second frame. Carl gets no points in the second frame for a cumulative score of 5 through the second frame.

Success Goal = outscore your opponent with as high a score as you can bowl

		Game number			
		1	2	3	4
Your Score	(points) =	_____	_____	_____	_____
Opponent's Score	(points) =	_____	_____	_____	_____

11. Battle

This game requires everyone to try his or her best, using a variety of strike- and spare-shooting skills.

Rules: Two teams compete against each other on a pair of lanes. Unlike regulation team competition, bowlers on a team participate together in only one single, regulation game line. The single game line on the odd lane is the odd team's score, and the single game line on the even lane is the even team's score.

Objective: To outscore the opposing team in a regulation game with the addition of special bonus points. Leadoff bowlers begin play by bowling on their respective lanes. The bowler from the odd team has starting honors and attempts to knock down a number of pins that he or she feels the leadoff bowler from the even team cannot match. Then the even team's leadoff bowler bowls, attempting to match the pinfall of the first leadoff bowler. It is not necessary to knock down more pins—just to match the pinfall.

If there is a match in pinfall count, the team on the even lane is awarded 20 bonus points to its score; if there is no match, the 20 bonus points are added to the odd team's score. Starting honors alternate between teams from frame to frame. In the second frame, the even team's second bowler bowls first, and the odd team's second bowler attempts to match the score. After the first balls, each bowler must try to convert his or her spares, because the base score is a regulation score. In a 10-frame game with 12 balls possible, there are 240 bonus points at stake.

Success Goal = complete 2 games of Battle, bowling the higher team point total

	Game 1	Game 2	Bonus	Total
Your Team's Score =	_____	_____	_____	_____
Opposing Team's Score =	_____	_____	_____	_____

12. *Bowling Bingo*

This version of the familiar Bingo game features first ball pinfall as the number to be entered into Bowling Bingo squares on a prepared scoresheet.

Scoresheet Preparation: A heavy line is drawn on the division between the fifth and sixth frames, and another heavy line is drawn between the fifth and sixth games (see Appendix B Scoresheet). The result is four "Bowling Bingo cards" consisting of 25 frames each. Mark the frames as shown in the Sample Scoresheet for Bingo.

Sample Scoresheet for Bingo

2-4	5-8	9-12	13-16	17-20
2	Free	10	14	20
4	7	12	16	Free
2	6	Free	15	17
Free	5	9	13	18
3	8	11	Free	19

Rules: The two teams on each pair of lanes join forces and compete against other paired teams. Teams on lanes 1 and 2 are called "Pair 1," those on lanes 3 and 4 are called "Pair 2," and so on. Each team pair uses one Bowling Bingo card for each game. Bowlers should not race; bowling proceeds at the usual pace and normal lane courtesy should be observed.

Every bowler on the teams participates in bowling only first balls to achieve pin count. Only first balls are rolled, and the remaining pins are then swept off the pindeck.

The number in the Bowling Bingo squares range from 2 to 20. The leadoff bowlers from both teams roll first balls, and the scorekeeper adds the two pinfall counts together. If this pinfall count total matches one of the numbers on the Bowling Bingo card, the scorekeeper crosses out the number with a heavy X. Only one occurrence of a number on a card may be crossed out per two-bowler attempt.

The next-up bowlers from both teams follow, rolling only first balls. The total of the two bowlers' first balls is compared with the Bowling Bingo card; the scorekeeper crosses out the next number. This rotation continues until a team pair has five X entries—either across, down, or diagonally—on its Bowling Bingo card.

When the team pair has "made Bingo," some (or all) of the members should shout, "Bingo!" At this point the game ends, and another game of Bowling Bingo (or a drill) may begin.

Variations: Additional patterns may be used to provide variety (see Example Bingo Patterns).

Example Bingo Patterns

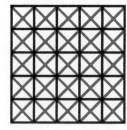
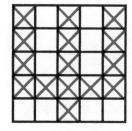
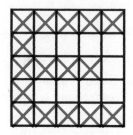
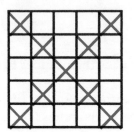
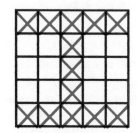
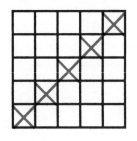
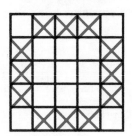

Success Goal = bowl 2 games of Bowling Bingo

Your Score = (#) _____ games of Bowling Bingo

13. Cutthroat Crossover

This is an amusing game of tactics to undermine the opponents. It also involves a variety of spare-shooting skills.

Rules: Two teams compete against each other on a pair of lanes. Unlike regulation team competition, all bowlers on a team participate together in bowling only one, single game line. The game line on the odd lane is the odd team's score, and the game line on the even lane is the even team's score.

The amusing feature of this game is that the leadoff bowler of one team bowls the first ball of the other team's leadoff bowler's frame! Then the next bowler from each team switches to the correct lane to try to pick up the spare.

Objective: To outscore the opposing team in a regulation single game. One important rule, though: A first ball rolled into the channel counts as a strike for the team in whose frame it was rolled, so a team should not try to low-ball the opposing team into a low score. It is advantageous to keep the ball on the lane. A sharpshooter might try for a corner pin, leaving nine pins for the opposition's spare. A daring first-ball bowler might even try to create a split, at the risk of high pinfall or even an inadvertent strike.

Success Goal = 2 games of Cutthroat Crossover, winning both

	Game 1	Game 2	Total
Your Team's Score =	_____	_____	_____
Opposing Team's Score =	_____	_____	_____

14. *Half-Pyramid*

This is another fun accuracy game that capitalizes on your spare-targeting ability. The objective is to cross out a half-pyramid of numbers on a specially prepared scoresheet by matching the numbers with first- and second-ball pin count. Prepare your scoresheet using the Sample Half-Pyramid Scoresheet.

Rules: Competition will be between two teams on a pair of lanes, each team with its own scoresheet and attempting to cross out all the numbers before the opposing team. Each team must begin at the bottom of the pyramid and work upward. A team wins the right to cross out a number if a bowler's first- and second-ball pinfall matches the number.

Success Goal = complete 2 games of Half-Pyramid, attempting to cross out all numbers before the opposing team

Your Score = (#) _____ games played

Sample Half-Pyramid Scoresheet

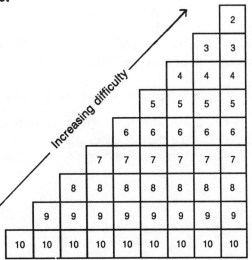

15. Tic-Tac-Bowl

This is another fun accuracy game that depends on the strike- and spare-targeting abilities of all participants. The objective is the same as the traditional Tic-Tac-Toe game—to get 3 X or O entries in a row, horizontally, vertically, or diagonally on the game board. The right to place an X or an O on the board is earned by making correct first- and second-ball attempts.

Rules: Competition is on a pair of lanes, with either individuals or teams (hereafter called players) competing against each other. Players assigned the X entries are called X players, or simply X; players assigned the O entries are called O players, or simply O. Players may either remain on one lane of the pair or alternate lanes.

Toss a coin to decide who starts first. Then, X and O alternates two balls, each attempting to get a strike. The first player to either get a strike or convert the spare, gets to place a mark on the Tic-Tac-Bowl board.

Success Goal = complete 3 or more games of Tic-Tac-Bowl, attempting to get 3 X or O entries horizontally, vertically, or diagonally on the game board

Your Score =

(#) _____ games played

(#) _____ games won

16. Bowling Golf

This drill combines the golf concept of shooting par with strike and spare skills. Each ''golfer'' uses a single regulation bowling game line but does not keep a regulation bowling score. Ten ''holes,'' or frames, constitute a round of Bowling Golf. Scoring is as follows:

- Double Strike: A strike after a previous strike is an ''eagle,'' or ''two under par'' for the frame in which the second strike is scored. This scoring represents a bonus; no additional bonus is given for 3 or more strikes.
- Strike: The score is a ''birdie,'' ''one under par,'' or ''minus one'' for the frame.
- Spare: The score for the frame is ''even'' or ''par.''
- Miss: Leaving one pin standing after two balls is a ''bogey,'' ''one over par,'' or ''plus one''; leaving two standing is a ''double bogey''; leaving three standing is a ''triple bogey,'' and so on.
- Converting a Split: Converting any split to a spare is a ''birdie,'' or ''minus one.''

Rules: Competition is on either a single lane or on a pair. If there are fewer than three persons assigned to a lane, the bowlers on a pair of lanes play against each other and alternate lanes. If more, bowlers on each lane compete among themselves on a single lane.

Sample scoring for three bowlers: The leadoff bowler starts the action with a strike (birdie); the score for his or her first frame is −1. The second bowler rolls his or her first frame, rolling a seven count and knocking down only one pin on the second attempt (double bogey); the score in the first frame is +2. The third bowler rolls next, getting a split that is converted into a spare (birdie); the resulting score is a −1.

In the second frame, the leadoff bowler gets another strike (an eagle), the second bowler gets a strike, and the third bowler gets a strike. In the third frame, the leadoff bowler gets a split and "eight out" (leaving two pins standing); the second bowler gets a spare; and the third bowler gets another strike. The score so far:

Bowler	1	2	3	Cumulative Total
Leadoff	−1	−2	+2	−1
Second	+2	−1	even	+1
Third	−1	−1	−2	−4

The third bowler is in the lead, three "strokes" ahead of the leadoff bowler and five strokes ahead of the second bowler.

Skins game variation: Award 5 points to the winner of an individual hole (frame). In case of a tie for hole winner, carry over the 5 points, adding them to the 5 winner's points on the next hole.

Success Goal =

a. complete 1 round of Bowling Golf, attempting to make the lowest score

b. Skins game: complete 1 round of golf, attempting to accumulate the greatest number of points

Your Score =

a. (#) _____ for 1 round of Bowling Golf

b. (#) _____ points for 1 Bowling Golf Skins game

Step 15 **Goal Setting**

In bowling, as in other sports, if you are to continue to improve you must continually set goals for yourself. *Goal setting* is the act of identifying a desire or objective for the purpose of attaining it; it usually involves a specific action statement of the goal in clear, unambiguous terms. For any goal to be effective in modifying behavior, it should have to be accomplished within a time limit or within a given set of attempts. Throughout this book the Keys to Success give you technique goals, while the Success Goals give you specific short-range performance goals.

WHY IS GOAL SETTING IMPORTANT?

Research in sport psychology and other disciplines indicates that regular goal setting can enhance your performance. Goal setting focuses your attention on the task, inducing more effort in competition as well as practice. Goals also make you more persistent and encourage experimentation with many, varied methods in search of superior ways to attain the goals. You can hinder your progress if you do not set goals, because you would have little or no idea about what to accomplish or how to accomplish it.

HOW TO SET GOALS

In general, for goals to be effective in directing your behavior toward their attainment, they must satisfy certain requirements. First, goals should be challenging but realistically attainable. Goals should be stated or set in such a manner that builds in probable success. You may adjust your goals down (make them easier) if necessary, or up (make them more difficult) at an appropriate time in your training. It is more beneficial to your progress to attain easy goals than to fail at attaining difficult goals. Little victories build your con-

fidence, helping you to think of yourself as a winner—even before you have actually won in competition.

Second, you should set *performance goals*, because these are more effective in improving skill than *outcome goals*. A performance goal involves the quality of execution or some intermediate accomplishment. For example, getting two strikes within 5 frames is a performance goal: It is under your direct control. Winning a tournament, however, is an outcome goal: It is not completely under your direct control.

Performance-oriented players—those who set performance goals—are more successful in attaining their goals than outcome-oriented players. Outcome-oriented players usually do not attain their goals, because outcome goals are loaded with built-in frustration. If you set your sights on good performance, though, satisfaction and a feeling of achievement are frequent, helping you improve rapidly. The following chart summarizes the characteristics of these two types of players:

Performance-oriented player	*Outcome-oriented player*
Sets performance goals	Sets outcome goals
Concerned with execution	Concerned with winning
Goals within control	Goals beyond control
Handles pressure well	Too anxious under pressure
More motivated	Less motivated
Eager goal-setter	May reject goal setting
Often successful	Less often successful
Judges self in terms of own successes	Judges self in terms of peer comparisons

You should use *short-range goals* as "stepping stones" to the attainment of *long-range goals*. For instance, the probability is very low that someone who has never piloted a plane before can take off, fly, and safely land one on the first attempt. However, if that person is instructed in the first technique involved in flying, then the second, then the third, and so on, the probability of making a safe, successful solo flight increases greatly.

A long-range goal such as bowling a 300 game implies a series of short-range goals, each one being to get a strike. Each short-range goal of getting a strike itself implies other short-range goals leading to its attainment: executing the setup, the approach, and the release properly. Proper execution leads to strikes; strikes lead to 300 games.

You should set only specific goals and strategies for attainment of a goal. Any specific, concretely analyzable goal is more effective in bringing about improvement than is a general, nonspecific one like doing one's best or bowling well in a certain week.

Finally, you should set only positive goals in an active voice. For example, the statement "I will make my next three spares" is more specific, encouraging, and attainable than "I will not miss spares." You may use either of two formats in formulating a goal:

(a) subject + action verb + object (as in the former statement) or
(b) "to" + action verb + object ("to make my next three spares").

The following orderly sequence of suggestions will help you develop effective goals and strategies:

1. Develop a clear idea of what you want to achieve. Prioritize your desires, asking yourself, "How important is this desire in relation to the others?" Then write down each goal on a separate piece of paper or a notecard, leaving space underneath for listing strategies leading to attainment of the goal.
2. Decide how you will attain your goals. Under each goal, write action statements that clearly indicate the strategies that will accomplish it. List the strategies in the order in which they should occur, and leave some space between them.
3. Decide how you will carry out each goal-directed strategy. List these tactics in order (prioritize them) as well, and leave space between them.
4. Regularly compare your performance with your original stated goals. Carry your list of goals and strategies with you so that you can read them often. Always know how you are progressing; such evaluation is absolutely necessary to promoting your continued effort and ultimate success. It's encouraging—every time you realize that you have attained a goal, you have told yourself that you are a success!
5. Provide yourself with a means of moral support. Associate only with positive-thinking persons who share your feelings about performance goals. You will have a difficult time applying yourself to the achievement of your goals if the significant others in your environment are not supportive or if they are outcome oriented. Associate with successful persons, and you yourself will have a better chance of becoming a success!

Goal-Setting Drills

1. Goal Development

Working with a partner, pick one or more goals from the "Sample List of Ultimate Goals" at the end of this drill and write this goal down on a piece of paper. Under your ultimate goal statement, write the short-range goals and strategies you will use to attain your ultimate goal. You may draw flowcharts to help you visualize how the goals and strategies relate to each other. Discuss your goals with your partner as you develop them. When you are through, check your goals against the criteria presented in the text, and record them under "Your Score."

Flowchart example: Start with an ultimate goal and work backward to determine what short-range goals are necessary in working toward it. Work backward from each short-range goal to develop strategies to attain it. Your flowchart may also be branched, with several goals not related to each other leading to the attainment of a single, ultimate goal. Many goal heirarchies are possible (see Figure 15.1a, b, c).

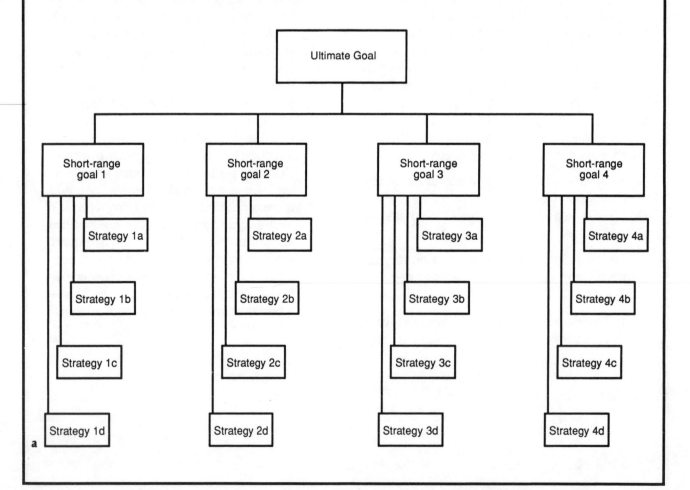

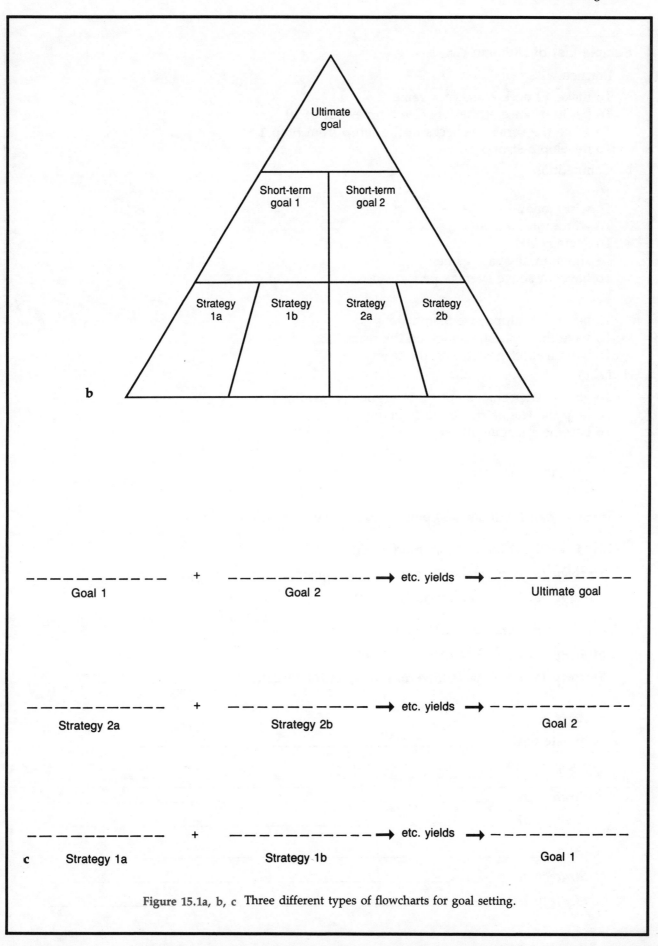

Figure 15.1a, b, c Three different types of flowcharts for goal setting.

Sample List of Ultimate Goals

a. Practice

To make 10 pocket hits in a game
To be on balance at the foul line 8 times out of 10
To recite the series of checks in the setup from Step 1
To develop a strong game

b. Competition

To win
To win money
To win a tournament
To average 200
To shoot an all-spare game
To have an above-average performance

c. Team

To become a supportive teammate
To have the highest average on the team
To bowl leadoff position on the team

d. League

To gain greater enjoyment from league competition
To help the league run more smoothly
To become a league officer

Success Goal = develop one or more ultimate goals

Example

Ultimate goal: I will bowl 20 pins higher in the next game.

Goal 1: I will hit the headpin more often.

Strategy 1a: I will make the appropriate adjustment in the setup.

Strategy 1b: I will concentrate more effectively on the shot.

Goal 2: I will make one more strike.

Strategy 1a: I will setup more carefully.

Strategy 1b: I will focus more intensely on the target.

Your Score =

a. **Ultimate goal** _____

   Goal 1 _____
   Strategy 1a _____
   Strategy 1b _____

   Goal 2 _____
   Strategy 2a _____
   Strategy 2b _____

or

b. Ultimate goal _____

   Goal 1 _____

     Strategy 1a _____

     Strategy 1b _____

   Goal 2 _____

     Strategy 2a _____

     Strategy 2b _____

2. *Personal Goal Development*

Write down 10 of your own ultimate goals in the spaces provided below. Transfer each to a sheet of paper, using one sheet for each of the 10 goals, and develop them as in Drill 1. Set challenging, but attainable, performance goals.

When you have finished developing 2 of your goals, show them to your instructor. After discussing your work with your instructor, finish developing the remaining 8 goals on your own.

When you are sure that your goals are specific and clearly stated, and that you have listed appropriate action strategies leading to their attainment, carry your goal sheets with you every time you bowl. If you go to a league session, carry your league-play goals; if you go to practice, carry your practice goals, and so on. May you have the best of luck in attaining your personal bowling goals.

Success Goal = 10 personal goals listed in the spaces below and developed on separate sheets of paper, checking your work against the criteria presented in the text.

Your Score =

  1. _____

  2. _____

  3. _____

  4. _____

  5. _____

  6. _____

  7. _____

  8. _____

  9. _____

 10. _____

3. Short-Range Goals

Develop five short-range goals that you want to be able to achieve during a game. Bowl 2 games, and record whether or not you achieved your goals.

Success Goal = 5 short-range goals developed and achieved

Your Score =

	Goal	Achieved Game 1	Achieved Game 2
1.	_____	_____	_____
2.	_____	_____	_____
3.	_____	_____	_____
4.	_____	_____	_____
5.	_____	_____	_____

Step 16   Practicing for Success

Practice is one of the most motivating aspects of bowling because it is during practice that you notice more keenly the changes taking place in your performance! Practice sessions are mirrors for seeing your success, providing frequent opportunities for you to see yourself accomplishing the short-range goals that lead to long-range improvements. Step 16 will help you learn some effective practice techniques.

TYPES OF PRACTICE

There are two general categories of practice: physical and mental.

Physical Practice

The three types of physical practice are unsupervised, or solo, practice; *reciprocal*, or *buddy-system*, practice; and supervised practice. Unsupervised practice is carried out by you alone, without feedback from any source other than from your internal feelings, your kinesthetic sense, and other self-observations, as well as from the results at the pins.

In reciprocal (buddy-system) practice, you are the performer and a partner is your observer; the roles are switched so you can help each other. Verbal feedback from the observer is the special added element. Although you and your buddy need not be of equal proficiency in bowling, it is beneficial if you share a common goal of desired improvement and have similar observation and concentration skills.

In supervised practice, you are evaluated by a skilled, experienced bowler, and some type of instruction is usually given. Therefore, supervised practice usually involves the services of someone more highly trained than your buddy-system observer, such as an instructor or a coach. Traditional one-on-one bowling instruction falls into this category.

Mental Practice

There is only one type of mental practice; mental imagery. It is usually carried out by you alone in a quiet, private atmosphere.

WHY IS PRACTICE IMPORTANT?

Any of the types of practice potentially improves your performance. Although practice alone does not guarantee perfection, you can be assured that performance will not improve without it. Intelligent practice is goal-oriented practice. Through appropriate goal setting and practicing of attainable goals, you take control of your own development, becoming more self-reliant, gaining confidence in your ability, and cultivating a healthy attitude toward the sport. If you practice correctly with well-defined goals, your performance will improve; if you practice incorrectly, either without goals or with erroneous goals, your performance will worsen.

Understand that improvement in your performance will probably not occur at a consistent, steady pace. Your progress will be marked by performance level *plateaus*, during which you may experience little improvement or even a lowering of your scores. Plateaus are not all bad, though: They indicate the time period during which new movement patterns are consolidated—being integrated within your neuromuscular system and becoming automatic. Be patient with yourself and practice intelligently, and you will see progress!

Why Use Types of Physical Practice?

Unsupervised practice is particularly important when you are learning new movements requiring thoughtful repetition. In order to train your neuromuscular system, you must be able to isolate yourself from distractions and concentrate deeply, focusing your thoughts on a specific body part's position or action.

Reciprocal practice is important because it provides you with accurate, instantaneous feedback from the observer. This timely feedback is very important because the feel associated with a given shot, which dissipates rapidly, is still fresh in your mind and muscles. To capture this feel with the help of the observer's verbal feedback, along with the visual feedback of seeing how the pins act, adds greatly to your ability to *shape* (purposefully modify) your performance. It is vital that the observer not be distracted from observing consistently. The observer should not give feedback without actually having paid attention to the shot; the absence of feedback is better than inaccurate feedback.

A high-quality supervised practice session is very beneficial because it focuses on the bowling fundamentals. Your instructor can rebuild your game on these sound basics, one part at a time. Such practice is most effective if each session presents you with no more than three new elements to work on.

When should you practice with trained supervision? You should do so when you would like to bowl better—not just to remove flaws from your technique; to do just the latter would be to accentuate the negative. You do not remove bad habits—you replace them with good habits! Do not take instruction before an important performance. The best time to restructure your technique is during the summer, a time during which you may forsake league competition for learning.

Why Use Mental Practice?

There is good evidence to show that you can mentally practice movements anytime and anywhere to improve actual performance. Mental practice involves your creating an experience in your "minds eye": Picture yourself taking your setup and approach, and delivering your ball to achieve a perfect result. In using mental practice, you are effectively running your movement plan without actually bowling. If you use mental practice on a regular basis, you will become more proficient at it—because you "live" each experience. You can use mental practice to help program proper technique and to correct problems and mistakes instead of hoping that such things will work themselves out.

The mental practice technique is based on *psychoneuromuscular theory*, which suggests that imagined events can cause firing of nerve impulses to the muscles involved in the imagined activity. Researchers believe that these impulses can make the body believe that it is actually participating in the activity, thereby strengthening the appropriate nerve pathways. Many top sport stars consistently use imagery to maintain superior performance. You may use imagery to ingrain smooth and flawless bowling movements into your performance techniques.

Because you may not be able to afford to physically practice as often as you like and because a bowling center may not be conveniently located, you should carry out mental practice at regular intervals. This is not to suggest that you can train yourself effectively with no actual physical practice; however, you can make faster progress if you regularly use both methods.

HOW TO EXECUTE PHYSICAL PRACTICE

Preparation: Give yourself a good opportunity to make progress in practice by taking control of your situation. Try to ensure the following:

1. Pick a remote lane on which to bowl. If you are practicing your physical game, remove yourself from as many distractions as possible. However, if you are working on your mental skills routine, you may want to challenge your ability to concentrate by bowling next to a noisy group.
2. Bowl on an hourly-rate basis if you must bowl a great number of games in a short period of time. If you need to practice slowly and deliberately, bowl on a per-game basis.
3. Do not keep a standard numerical score. The quality of your technique cannot

often be determined from your score, which is frequently a poor indicator of progress. If your score is kept by some sort of automatic scoring device, do not pay attention to it. You may keep some sort of score on paper, though, if directed to do so in one of the drills in this book.

4. Know precisely what you want to practice—have it written down in the form of a performance-oriented goal, with strategies leading to its attainment. If you are using the buddy system to practice, it is desirable that both of you have received instruction at the same time from the same instructor.

5. Always take some type of warm-up, preferably within 5 minutes of beginning to bowl. Warm-ups are essential in any sport because they help prepare you mentally as well as physically.

Conducting practice: Structure your practice session in accordance with the following suggestions. This procedure applies to both unsupervised and supervised practice. Do not engage in idle conversation until you reach the final point.

1. Take 5 to 10 shots to attain the proper feel before attempting to align yourself for a strike. If you are not executing your shot properly (i.e., if you do not feel unhurried, in rhythm, and unforced), trying to line up for your first ball shot is useless.

2. Align yourself for your strike ball. Only when you are hitting your target line consistently can you truly fine-tune your delivery.

3. Begin to work on your goal. Your goal may be to complete one or more of the solo drills in this book; if so, follow all directions very closely. If your goal is general refinement of technique, concentrate on making a flowing motion with proper execution on every shot. If your goal is correction of a faulty facet of your game (like poor hand position, torso instability, bending your knees at the wrong moment, etc.), focus your selective attention strongly on only the body parts involved. Always note what effects varying an execution facet has on your ball's path, which is a good source of feedback. Note that a change to better technique usually increases your leverage, requiring you to realign your strike target line.

4. Write down all important, useful information in your notes. If you are using the buddy system, include your observer's feedback. Take your notes home and think about them. Resolve what needs to be done prior to your next practice session; for instance, you may need to improve your ball fit, buy a new pair of shoes, or review your target lines.

   Log any and all indications of progress; no matter whether objective or subjective. Such entries in your notes represent little, but clear, victories that build your confidence, helping to make your attitude toward practice more positive and your outlook on your entire game more optimistic. Use these notes to revise your list of performance-oriented goals.

5. End the practice session when appropriate. When you are tired, stop practicing. When you are performing poorly for any reason and cannot seem to make the correct movements, stop! Do not allow yourself to practice poor performance!

   If you must quit but are not tired, make a few more of the correct movements to ingrain them before you stop; this will allow you to quit on the upswing. If you are performing well and are not tired, try to continue bowling as long as you can to further refine the correct movements.

   If you are using the buddy system, the time to switch roles is when the performer is tired, allowing him or her to rest and observe the other member of the buddy team. It is best not to switch roles until the performer has deeply sensed the results of a properly executed shot; it should be locked into the mind and muscles before he or she stops.

6. Put away your equipment properly and use a cool-down. Relax for a short period before beginning a new activity.

HOW TO EXECUTE MENTAL PRACTICE

Confine yourself in a quiet room, either in a comfortable chair or in a reclining position. Use a progressive muscle relaxation technique to relax your body while you clear and quiet your thoughts.

Close your eyes and envision yourself in great detail going through the motions of your setup and a successful delivery terminating with a successful result, either a strike or a spare. Make your image as vivid as possible; experience all of the sights, sounds, smells, and other sensations normally associated with a real practice setting. Repeat your imaged delivery, bowling as many games as you can in the time you allot yourself. You may keep score on a notepad if desired.

Practice Drills

1. Charting Progress: Unsupervised Practice

This drill shows you how to use a scoresheet to record your performance when practicing alone. Obtain a regular scoresheet. If your score is kept by an automatic scoring device, make a scoresheet for yourself. Do not keep score in the conventional manner. Rather, you should record the following types of information (the examples are for a right-handed bowler):

a. *Type of strike*: As the game progresses, write "P" for a solid pocket hit, "M" for a light mixer or shaker (a pocket hit in which the headpin rebounds off the side wall or kickboard), "4" for a slow 4-pin topple, "W" for a "weak 10" hit (the 10 pin barely topples), "B" for a Brooklyn hit, and so on in the appropriate frame spaces.

b. *Pins left standing*: List them from the lowest to the highest number—the 2-4-5, or the *bucket* (2-4-5-8), or a *washout* (1-2-4-10), and so on.

c. *Ball used during the game*: Describe this in the left half of the game line space reserved for your name.

d. *Line played*: Use the right half of the name space to indicate the target line you are playing during the game, such as 13-10 or 12-11.

e. *Write anything else of value (below the respective frame)*: How you felt, whether you pulled the ball, and so on.

A game annotated in this fashion may look like the Sample Self-Scorecard. The results of your shots are recorded within the frame boxes, while comments regarding your performance are written below the respective boxes. You can learn something about the quality of your approach and delivery in each frame by studying your notations. Such scoresheets may be especially useful in helping to determine skills that need extra attention.

Sample Self-Scorecard

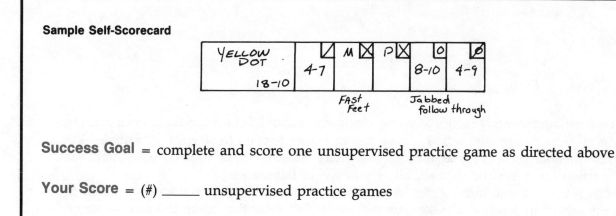

Success Goal = complete and score one unsupervised practice game as directed above

Your Score = (#) _____ unsupervised practice games

2. *Charting Progress: Supervised Practice*

This drill shows you how to use a scoresheet to record your performance when practicing while being observed by a partner (buddy), an instructor, or a coach. Your observer should prepare the scoresheet and make entries as directed in the previous drill, recording only information relevant to your execution and pinfall results. Your observer should write down information such as

1. type of strike,
2. pins left standing,
3. ball used during the game, and,
4. line played, as well as that which you could not be expected to know, including
   - the actual path that the ball followed; this will not always be the same as the target line (the line played) you elected to use at the start of the game,
   - early, late, or in-time pushaway,
   - early, late, or in-time ball at the release,
   - bending over too far at the waist, and
   - any other relevant information that only an observer can see.

In the Sample Observer Scorecard, the results of your shots are recorded in the frame boxes, while the observer's comments are written below the respective boxes. Such scoresheets help you give attention to skills that you may neglect because it is difficult to detect them on your own.

Sample Observer Scorecard

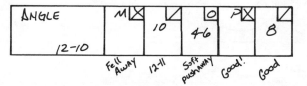

Success Goal = complete 1 supervised practice game

Your Score = (#) _____ supervised practice games

3. Mental Practice

You may conduct mental practice anytime or anywhere, but it is best conducted in a peaceful setting. You may mentally ''bowl'' three games before you go to sleep, for example. You may also mentally bowl a game during a rest break. See the ''How to Execute Mental Practice'' section for directions. (Do *not* allow yourself to fall asleep.)

Just as if you were running a film in your mind, close your eyes and watch yourself repeatedly take your setup and make only successful deliveries that result in success—strikes or spares. Repeat your mental shots over and over, bowling a 3-game series. Keep score on a notepad.

Success Goal = complete a 3-game series of mental practice

Your Score = (#) _____ games of mental practice

Rating Your Total Progress

After completing the steps in this book, it is time to evaluate your progress. To the right of each question, check the column that best describes you or your performance.

BACKGROUND KNOWLEDGE EVALUATION

Do you feel comfortable around other bowlers and in conversation with bowlers of all skill levels? Rate yourself objectively on your working knowledge of the following concepts associated with bowling.

Do you know	Yes	No
how bowling emerged as a competitive sport?	___	___
the relative dimensions of the approach, the lane, and related bowling equipment?	___	___
the meaning of bowling terms as defined in the glossary?	___	___
how to keep score, including score index?	___	___

Checks in any category other than yes tell you to review and study the corresponding concepts. If all of your checks are in the yes category, congratulations! This indicates your potentially high level of confidence in a bowling environment!

PHYSICAL SKILLS EVALUATION

Do you feel that you have an effective physical game? Rate yourself honestly on the following physical skills.

	Excellent	Good	Average	Poor
Executing the setup and the four-step delivery	___	___	___	___
Rolling effective straight and hook balls	___	___	___	___
Targeting effectively for strikes	___	___	___	___
Targeting effectively for spares	___	___	___	___
Practicing effectively	___	___	___	___

Checks in any category other than "Excellent" tell you to work on the corresponding items. Congratulations if you got all excellent ratings!

MENTAL SKILLS EVALUATION

Do you maintain effective mental control in game situations? Rate yourself honestly on the following mental skills; assume that all statements apply only to competitive bowling.

	Always	Sometimes	Seldom	Never	Unaware
Setting realistic performance goals that lead to improvement	_____	_____	_____	_____	_____
Avoiding tendency to tense up	_____	_____	_____	_____	_____
Controlling my anger quickly	_____	_____	_____	_____	_____
Sustaining a high level of concentration	_____	_____	_____	_____	_____
Using a progressive muscle relaxation technique	_____	_____	_____	_____	_____
Making positive self-statements	_____	_____	_____	_____	_____
Visualizing myself making perfect shots before I make an actual shot	_____	_____	_____	_____	_____
Talking only when necessary	_____	_____	_____	_____	_____

Checks in any category other than ''Always'' indicate that you should work on the corresponding skills. Congratulations if you rated yourself ''Always'' on all items. You are in control!

ATTITUDE EVALUATION

Do you gain true satisfaction from bowling? Rate your present attitude toward bowling by responding to the following statements.

	Always	Sometimes	Seldom	Never	Unaware
Looking forward to my next bowling session	_____	_____	_____	_____	_____
Believing that bowling is only an extension of myself, not having a bowling obsession	_____	_____	_____	_____	_____
Studying bowling between sessions	_____	_____	_____	_____	_____
Mentally practicing between sessions	_____	_____	_____	_____	_____
Keeping a record of all of my scores	_____	_____	_____	_____	_____
Talking about bowling with others	_____	_____	_____	_____	_____
Helping other bowlers when asked to do so	_____	_____	_____	_____	_____
Believing that my performance will steadily improve through my own application and effort	_____	_____	_____	_____	_____
Feeling that I may experience something new at my next bowling session	_____	_____	_____	_____	_____
Feeling that I may beat my previous best performances during my next bowling session	_____	_____	_____	_____	_____

Checks in any category other than "Always" indicate some degree of confusion or dissatisfaction with the corresponding aspect of bowling. Congratulations if you now derive satisfaction and enjoyment from bowling!

OVERALL BOWLING PROGRESS

Considering all of the preceding factors, how would you rate your bowling progress?

____ Very successful

____ Successful

____ Barely successful

____ Unsuccessful

How pleased are you with your progress?

____ Very pleased

____ Pleased

____ Not pleased

In what level of bowling do you hope to participate in the future?

____ League and tournament play

____ Occasional recreational play

____ None

Appendix A

Individual Program

INDIVIDUAL COURSE IN _____ GRADE/COURSE SECTION _____

STUDENT'S NAME _____ STUDENT ID # _____

SKILLS/CONCEPTS	TECHNIQUE AND PERFORMANCE OBJECTIVES	WT* ×	POINT PROGRESS** =				FINAL SCORE***
			1	2	3	4	

Note. From "The Role of Expert Knowledge Structures in an Instructional Design Model for Physical Education" by J.N. Vickers, 1983, *Journal of Teaching in Physical Education*, **2**(3), p. 17. Copyright 1983 by Joan N. Vickers. Adapted by permission.

*WT = Weighting of an objective's degree of difficulty.

**PROGRESS = Ongoing success, which may be expressed in terms of (a) accumulated points (1, 2, 3, 4); (b) grades (D, C, B, A); (c) symbols (merit, bronze, silver, gold); (d) unsatisfactory/satisfactory; and others as desired.

***FINAL SCORE equals WT times PROGRESS.

Appendix B

Scoresheet

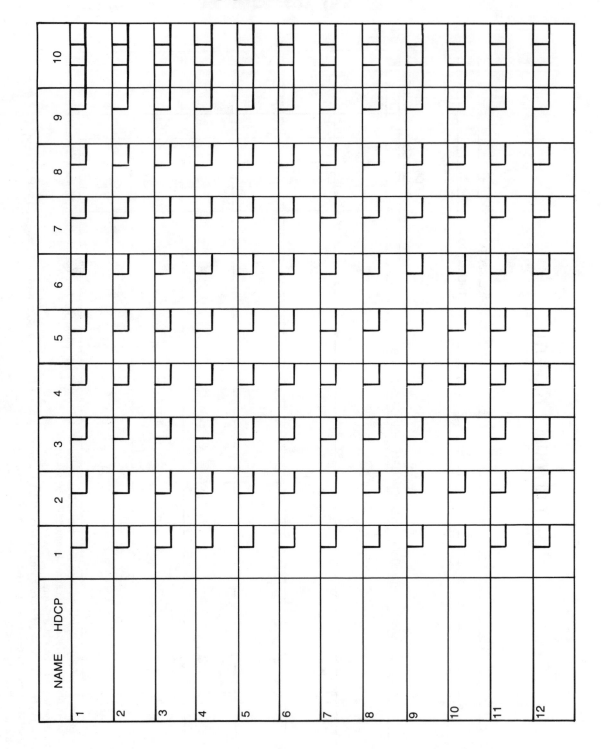

action Movement of a body part; also the movement of the pins after ball impact.

address Stance position; see **setup**.

alignment Positioning of the swing or approach relative to a target or a line.

alley Playing surface for bowling.

angle of attack Angle at which the ball rolls into the rack of pins.

approach Taking steps and swinging the ball during the delivery; area on which a bowler takes steps in delivering the ball.

approach line Line over which the center of the body moves during the approach.

axis of rotation Line through the center of the ball, around which the ball rotates while rolling.

backswing Portion of the swing starting at the lowest point in the downswing and ending with the ball at its highest point behind the bowler.

backup ball Ball that veers from the bowler's inside to the outside.

balance arm Arm opposite the bowling (swingside) arm.

balance side Portion of the bowler's body, the lane, or the approach on the same side as the nonbowling (balance) arm.

ball track Area on the surface of a bowling ball over which it rolls; area on the lane surface where frequent ball contact causes wear.

base score Arbitrary score from which handicap may be calculated.

be snooty Keeping the head back, looking at visual target out of the bottoms of the eyes, and following the visual target only with the eyes, not with the head.

bowling hand or **arm** Hand or arm with which the bowler rolls the ball.

break point Location down the lane at which a bowler's ball visibly begins to hook.

Brooklyn Refers to the strike ball; a hit on the side of the headpin opposite the bowling hand.

bumpout swing Backswing that moves away from the center of the body.

carry Extent to which a ball tends to strike; also knocking down a particular pin, for example, to carry the 7 pin.

channel Trough, or gutter, on each side of a lane.

checkpoint Each characteristic evaluated in a check sequence.

check sequence Orderly series of checks performed on any system; for example, checks on the setup, the steps, the grip.

chop To knock down the front pins in a spare leave while leaving the back pins standing.

clear Term specifically applied to the fingers during the release of the ball; exiting the grip hole without restriction.

clip Stopping the ball on its way to the top of the backswing.

conventional grip Ball grip in which both fingers are inserted to the second joints.

convergent swing Swing plane directed toward the front center of the bowler.

convert Knocking down all pins left standing after the first-ball attempt of a frame; making a spare.

cover To make a spare; to hit all pins of a spare leave with the ball; the outside layer in a bowling ball's construction.

curve ball A shot that travels a curved path to the pins from the bowler's outside to the inside but which shows no definite break point.

delivery Rolling the ball down the lane.

divergent swing Swing plane directed toward the front outside of the bowler.

downswing Portion of the bowler's swing starting at the extended pushaway position and ending with the ball at its lowest point as it is moving back.

dumped shot Lack of finger lift in delivering the ball, usually caused by the ball being early relative to the footwork.

dynamics Collective movement of objects in motion.

early pushaway Pushaway of the ball occurring before movement of the swingside foot.

error Failure of frame's second ball to knock down all the pins left standing by the first ball; performance of an action other than that desired.

extension setup Ball being held at the extended pushaway position.

fast feet Steps being taken at a pace faster than the cadence of the pendululm swing.

fast lane A low-friction lane on which it is difficult to roll a hook ball.

find a line To systematically adjust the target line and stance position until the ball is hitting the pocket.

finger inserts Plastic or rubber liners within the fingerholes, which allow a snug fit and greater traction.

fingers in the shot Feeling the fingers lift the ball, imparting roll or rotation at the release.

fingertip Ball grip in which both fingers are inserted to the first joints.

finish Last-step-and-slide stage of the delivery.

following the ball down Leaning the torso forward as the ball is moving into the downswing.

forward swing Portion of the bowler's swing starting at the top of the backswing and ending at the release point.

foul Any part of the bowler's body touching any part of the bowling establishment beyond the foul line during an otherwise legal delivery of the ball.

foul line Line that separates the approach from the lane.

frame   Unit division of a game of bowling that allows for two attempts at knocking down a full rack of pins.

full-roller   Ball that bears a track equal to its full circumference.

handicap   Pins added in an attempt to equalize one bowler's score with another's.

headpin   Pin at the front of the rack of pins.

high hit   Ball contacts the front pin of a full rack or a spare combination too fully.

hoist   "Adding to" the pendulum action of the backswing with muscular tension, resulting in a higher than desired backswing.

hook ball   Shot that follows a bent path to the pins from the bowler's outside to the inside.

hooking lane   Lane with a high-friction condition.

illegal pinfall   Pinfall resulting from any of the following: a ball which has left the lane surface before reaching the pins, a ball rebounding from the rear cushion, pins knocked down but returning to a standing position, pins touched by the pinsetter before they fall.

impact board   Specific term referring to the lane board number over which the ball rolled as it made contact with the pins.

impact point   General term denoting the point of ball contact with the pins.

inside   Portion of the bowler's body, the lane, or the approach that is on the same side as the balance arm; see **balance side**.

kickboard   Wall on either side of the rack of pins, from which they can rebound.

kingpin   5 pin.

lane condition   State of friction of the lane.

lane courtesy   Protocol in which bowlers on adjacent lanes or lane pairs may take orderly turns in rolling balls.

lane dressing   Oil applied over the lane finish to reduce wear by the ball.

lane finish   Tough plastic (urethane, lacquer, etc.) coating applied to seal and protect the bare lane surface.

late pushaway   Pushaway of the ball occurring after movement of the swingside foot has already begun.

league   Form of organized competition, with winners usually determined at the end of a 9-month bowling season.

leave   Any pins left standing after the first-ball attempt in a frame.

legal delivery   Ball leaves the bowler's hand and touches the lane past the foul line.

lift   To impart roll or rotation to a bowling ball with the bowling fingers.

light hit   Any first-ball attempt in which the ball barely touches the headpin to the outside.

line bowling   Aiming method that uses an imaginary line.

loft   To deliver a ball too far out onto the lane surface, usually caused by bending the thumb in the thumbhole.

low friction   Relative term describing a tendency for two touching surfaces to slide over each other.

make   To knock down all pins standing; one makes a strike or a spare.

mark   Either a spare or a strike, all 10 pins being knocked down in a frame.

match play   Competitive event in which the winner is determined by number of games won, not by the game scores.

medal play   Competitive event in which the winner is determined by game scores.

mental imagery   Willful, detailed imagining of persons, places, events, sensations, feelings.

mental practice   Repetitious rehearsal of an activity in the mind.

midline ball setup   Holding the ball at waist-level with both hands.

miss   see **error**.

negative axis pole   End of ball's axis of rotation farther away from the headpin; the outside pole.

next-up position   Recommended body position and location taken immediately before stepping up onto the approach.

one-step delivery   Exercise used by a bowler to practice the last-step-and-slide stage of the delivery.

opening up   Movement of the bowling shoulder toward the back, away from the target.

open play   Unscheduled casual bowling.

outside   Portion of the bowler's body, the lane, or the approach on the same side as the bowling arm; see **swingside**.

overlearn   To drill on a procedure until it becomes automatic.

parallel line bowling   Targeting system involving a logical relationship between the ball path and the path of the footwork.

pendulum   Weight suspended from a fixed point and swinging freely under only the action of gravity.

percentage difference handicap   Number of pins added to the score of the lower-average bowler based on the difference between his or her average and that of the bowler being competed against.

percentage from base score handicap   Number of pins added to the score of a bowler based on the difference between his or her average and a base score, for example, 200, 210, 220, and so on.

pick up   See **make**.

pin action   Movement of the pins after ball impact.

pin bowling   Using the pins as a visual target during the delivery.

pin count   Number of pins knocked down.

pin deck   Area of the lane on which the rack of 10 pins is set.

pinfall   Pins knocked down.

pitch   Amount of deviation of the axis of a hole away from or toward the geometric center of the ball.

placement distance   Distance in boards between the approach line and the target line, or between the body's center of gravity and the plane of the swing.

playing lanes   Adjustment of the target line to keep the ball impact point at the strike pocket.

pocket Desired point of ball impact for a strike; the 17th board.

pocket spare Any spare leave which can be made using the strike ball target line.

positive axis pole End of the ball's axis of rotation closer to the headpin; the inside pole.

progressive relaxation Systematic procedure for willfully relaxing the body.

projection Lifting the ball up and out and onto the lane surface with the fingers.

pulled shot Too much lift in delivering the ball, usually caused by a late ball.

pushaway Horizontal movement of the ball from its position in the setup to the pushaway destination.

pushaway destination Location in the swing plane that allows both elbows to be locked and the ball to be moved horizontally from its setup location—never down.

push the ball To push the ball straight out in the pushaway so that both elbows are locked; the bowling arm is thus completely straight before the ball moves down into the swing.

rack of pins All 10 pins set in a regulation tenpin formation.

Rangefinders® Collective system of dots and arrows on the approach and lane.

raw score Actual score of a game before handicap or points are added.

release Letting go of the ball during the slide, preferably with the thumb first, followed by the fingers.

reverse hook Ball that veers from the bowler's inside to the outside; see **backup ball.**

rolling Rotation around a horizontal axis, along a vertical plane; end-over-end motion of the ball proceeding in the direction of the pins; a rolling ball moves forward exactly 27 inches in a single revolution.

rotation Movement of any mass moving around an axis; for example, roll, spin.

rounding off the pushaway Failure to completely push the ball horizontally into the swing plane.

runway Portion of the lane on which the steps are taken; the approach.

Scotch doubles Two-person team competition in which one bowler bowls the first ball of a frame and the partner bowls the second.

scratch Score to which no handicap or points are added; a raw score.

semiroller Ball that bears a track approximately two thirds of the circumference of the ball.

settee Seating area behind each pair of lanes.

setup Phase of the delivery before initiation of movement.

setup area General location on the approach in which the setup is taken.

shot See **delivery.**

shuffling steps Failure to lift the feet sufficiently high off of the approach during the delivery.

sitting tall Ideal finish position at the foul line, keeping the back upright (no more than 20 degrees of forward lean) while the hips are lowered by bending the knees.

skidding Slipping motion of a ball as it proceeds toward the pins; a skidding ball moves forward more than 27 inches a single revolution.

slick lane Low-friction lane on which the ball tends not to hook.

sliding foot Foot on the side opposite the swing.

slow lane High-friction lane on which the ball hooks readily.

span Distance between the edges of the thumbhole and a fingerhole.

spare Second ball's knocking down all pins left standing after the first-ball attempt of a frame.

spin Rotation around a vertical axis; along a horizontal plane.

spinner Ball that bears a track that is one third or less of the circumference of the ball.

split Pins, other than the headpin, left standing with pins missing in between after the first-ball attempt; designated by an open circle.

spot bowling Use of a point on the lane as a visual target.

stance See **setup.**

stay behind the ball To keep the hand behind the ball and in line with the plane of the swing.

stay down To keep down the hips, not the head, in the finish; see **sitting tall.**

straight ball Ball that travels a straight path to the pins.

strike Knocking down all 10 pins with the first-ball attempt in a frame; designated with an X.

supporting fingers Fingers on the bowling hand that are not put into the grip holes.

sweep bar Bar on the pinsetting machine that pulls the pins into the area behind the pindeck.

swing plane Entire area bounded by the path of a bowler's swing; it may be termed a *solid circle.*

swingside Portion of the bowler's body, the lane, or the approach on the same side as the bowling arm; see **outside.**

swingside arm or **hand** Arm or hand with which the bowler rolls the ball.

takeaway Moving the balance arm out, back, and down from the pushaway destination at the same speed as the ball.

target-line bowling Targeting system involving two points of reference for a desired ball path and an appropriate path for the footwork to ensure delivery of the ball over the two points.

target point Desired place where the ball rolls across the arrows.

targeting system Orderly procedure for aligning the body with a desired ball path.

test target line Any known target line along which a ball is rolled to test the hooking characteristic of a lane.

topweight Weight added during manufacturing to an undrilled bowling ball to balance the ball after the holes are drilled.

touchdown   Place on the lane surface where the ball makes initial contact during the delivery; the first point designated along a target line.

touchdown point   Place where the ball should cross the foul line.

tournament   Organized competition among bowlers, with winners usually determined at the end of a single event.

translate a spare   To envision any spare leave as a simpler one.

trial swing   Swinging a ball to test it for appropriate weight.

visual target   Place on the lane on which to fix the gaze during the delivery.

washout   Headpin and other pins left standing after the first ball of a frame, with pins missing between them.

wraparound swing   Backswing that moves toward the center of the body.

References

Allen, G. (1986). *The Bowling industry study*. Tempe, AZ: Tempe Publishers.

Allen, G., & Ritger, D. (1981). *The complete guide to bowling strikes*. Tempe, AZ: Tempe Publishers.

Ritger, D., & Allen, G. (1978). *The complete guide to bowling spares*. Tempe, AZ/River Falls, WI: Ritger Sports.

Strickland, R. (1980). *Perceptive bowling*. Duncanville, TX: Professional Sports Services.

Weber, D., & Alexander, R. (1981). *Weber on bowling*. Englewood Cliffs, NJ: Prentice-Hall.

About the Author

Robert H. (Bob) Strickland, a bowler since 1958, won the first of his many championships in 1961. In 1978 he joined the Professional Bowlers Association, and he began teaching the sport professionally in 1983.

In addition to teaching bowling, Bob writes about the sport. He is the author of *Perceptive Bowling* and has been a guest columnist for the *National Bowlers Journal*. He also writes "Perceptive Bowling Tips," a nationally syndicated newspaper column on bowling instruction.

In 1986 Bob established the "Perceptive Bowling Clinic Successful Performance" course—a team-taught, comprehensive, and concentrated course for bowlers of all skill levels. He currently offers private bowling in-struction and conducts seminars and work-shops on various aspects of the sport, from youth coaching to bowling center marketing. He is a certified Young American Bowling Alliance Coach/Instructor and a member of the Bowling Writers Association of America, World Bowling Writers, and the Sigma Xi honorary research fraternity.

Bob was born in San Mateo, California, and grew up in Dallas, Texas. He holds degrees from the University of Texas at Arlington and the University of Georgia. Bob lives in Dallas with his wife, Sue, and is self-employed as a technical writer and marketing consultant. In his leisure time he enjoys music and reading.